Tom aged 6.

A Country Boy

Tom Lynam

**Stories & Reminiscences of a Young Man's
Journey from Mullingar to 1930's Dublin**

SL

Published by Siobhán Lynam
77 Christchurch View, Dublin 8. Ireland.
Email:siobhanlynam@iol.ie

First edition published in hardback as a special limited edition (twelve copies) Christmas 2003.

This paperback edition first published in August 2004.
Reprinted December 2004.

Editing, typesetting and layout: Siobhán Lynam.
Cover design and photo layout: Barrie Dowdall.
Photographs: Tom Lynam and friends with his brownie camera, unless otherwise acknowledged.
Printed in Ireland by Temple Printing Co. Ltd, Athlone, Co Westmeath.

British Library Cataloguing in Publication Data.
A catalogue record for this book is available from the British Library.

ISBN 0-9548211-0-6

Acknowledgements

I would like to acknowledge my family, my relatives and all my many dear friends who have been such an important part of my life and who are a part of my story.

I particularly want to say a big thanks to Siobhán who went to great pains to record and write up and publish my stories and reminiscences.

Thanks to all the people who so warmly encouraged us to make the stories available to others and to take the stories to a place that I would never have imagined. There are so many of these kind people, it is not possible to list them. A very special thanks to Westmeath Community Development Limited and the LEADER+ Programme and to Mullingar Credit Union for part-funding the first print run. Thanks to James Keane and Jonathan Mason for technical advice, to Barrie for all his talents and to Ailish for proofing this edition.

For my children

Marèse, Siobhán, Áine, Tomás, Ailish and Ciarán,

and my grandchildren

Niamh, Bianca, Conor and Meave.

The book is dedicated to

my darling Treasa, my lovely rose of Clare
and the love of my life

and to

my Mother, who gave me a great start in life
with her love, patience and kindness.

This is worth remembering:

I live for those who love me
For those who know me through
For the Heaven that smiles above me
And awaits my spirit too
For all human ties that bind me
For the task my God assigned me
For the bright hopes left behind me
And the good that I can do.

I live to learn their story
Who suffered for my sake
To emulate their glory
And follow in their wake
Bards, martyrs, and patriots
Nobles and sages of all ages
Whose deeds crowd history's pages
And whose times great volumes make.

I live for those who love me
For those who know me through
For the Heaven that smiles above me
And awaits my spirit too
For all human ties that bind me
For the task my God assigned me
For the bright hopes left behind me
And the good that I can do.

For the cause that lacks assistance
For the wrong that needs resistance
For the future in the distance
And the good that I can do.

I learned that, well I heard it, and I was just interested in it, and I just learned it off by heart. I thought there was an awful lot in it. As someone said it's all there and if that's your motto you'll have no problem.

When I look back, even as far back as my childhood, what do I think is the most important thing for me? Just get up in the morning and do the best you can. But I do think there's that part too *For the task my God assigned me.... and the good that I can do*

Mother at the pump that gave us the lovliest of spring water.

THE DAY THAT I WAS BORN WAS A GREAT DAY

I was told that I was born at home on the farm at Marlinstown on 25 September 1918, that was 86 years ago this year. It was a little over a month before the end of the First World War.

The day that I was born was a great day. The weather had been so good, and was so good that day that they cut and saved the corn all on the one day. In other words, the corn was crisp dry. On other occasions they would cut the corn, let it dry naturally, tie it in sheaves, it would be stucked[1] and stacked. But it was cut and stacked on the one day, on that day that I was born. That was one of the big things they all talked about. And I know where it happened. It was in the furrow field.

I was the third child. Josie was the eldest, then Pat, then myself. Of course, after me there was Bill, then Jim and Rose, Mary and Teresa. I don't remember where I was born, or who delivered me. I was called Thomas Ignatius after my Uncle Thomas, the Christian Brother.

There was a lady, I think she lived in Mullingar, three or four miles away, Mrs Cox I think was her name, and she'd come out with her bag, we wouldn't know anything about it but we'd be told afterwards, that you'd a baby brother or sister or whatever. The only one, or time, that I remember was when Teresa was born, 'cause we had to take the other children out in their prams and mind them and look after them, God help us.

The first thing I remember is burning the leg off a three-legged stool, when I was three years old. I burned the middle out of the leg.

---

[1] When the corn or oats crop was cut it was first 'stucked'. This meant standing about 10 sheaves upright to dry them. Later they would be stacked, a greater number of sheaves were bundled together and were left to further dry. When they were crisp dry, the corn would be brought into the haggard and then left there till the day of the treshing, when the treshing mill arrived.

THE FARMING BACKGROUND

The farm at home in Marlinstown was part of a bigger farm where all my father's family were reared. There were thirteen children in my father's family. His father, Patrick Lynam, my grandfather, originally came up from Porterstown to buy a farm. He had the option of buying two different estates but decided to buy the farm, which was furthest in from the public road. The farm would have been about 140 acres. I'm told my grandfather had been to America and came back with enough money to buy the farm[2].

Don't forget that my father Bill and all belonging to him went to the Christian Brothers. But my grandparents were told to keep my father at home, although the teachers told them that he was the brightest of all his family, he had brains to burn and he could learn if he wanted to. All the others went on in school, his sister Liz went off to school in Germany and then became a governess to a princess in Austria, she later married Uncle John McCormack; another sister, Aunt Paul was all we knew her by, was a nun in Navan; then there was Aunt Anne, she married a publican in Mullingar; Aunt Mary married Thomas Cunningham, a farmer from Derryconner, Ballivor; and Aunt Brigid (Biddy) McKeown married a farmer and publican from Rathwire in Killucan. Two of my father's brothers became Christian Brothers, Tom became Br. Ignatius (I was called after him) and James became Br. Clement. Another brother Uncle Mike (he was married to Aunt Agnes) was a publican in Mullingar. Uncle Pat married Aunt Bridie.

The land was divided after my grandfather died, between my father Bill and his brother Pat. Each other member of the family got twenty or thirty pounds, it was the women's dowry. According to the will of my grandfather, my own father was not allowed to marry until he was over thirty. It meant the others were protected by the will. I have a copy of the will at home.[3] Eventually they all bailed out and got whatever was coming to them, a few shillings, a few pounds and everyone was happy and eventually the farm was divided between my father and my Uncle Pat, his brother. There were two houses on the original

---

[2] Patrick Lynam was born in 1829. He went to the US with his brother Tom and returned around 1862. In 1865, 36 year old Patrick married 22 year old Anne Keenan. They had 13 children and he died in 1899 aged 70. According to the family tree, three of their children died at a young age, Anne at 2 years, Kate at 13 years and their last child Matt at 2 years. The Lynam Family Tree was prepared by Robert Cullen of Ennis Co. Clare. Robert is also a descendant of Patrick Lynam. A number of other people contributed to the research.

[3] Patrick Lynam's Will is outlined at the back of the book.

My father and mother, Bill Lynam & Mary Loughrey.

Mother and Father with relatives from Killucan. I am in the arms of the man on the left.
Pat is standing beside my mother and Bill is the other child in arms.

farm. One of the houses was the old herd's house, the house of the man that looked after the estate. Afterwards, we lived close to each other. Uncle Pat married Aunt Bridie and they had two children Paideen (Patrick Oliver) and Nancy. Paideen still lives in Marlinstown.

My parents met at a sports, Crookedwood sports, that would be half way between Mullingar and Castlepollard – really beautiful country. Crookedwood was a well-known sports at that time. Sports at that time I suppose, and when I was growing up, would be for all ages, with a whole list of various things: 100 yards race, high jump, shot and throwing weights. A weight of stone, that would be normally used for weighing corn would have some rope tied in the ring in the weight. It would weigh fifty-six pounds,[4] or a half hundredweight, and the men would swing it or throw it and there would be someone there to mark the ground where it landed. And there would be bicycle races too, there would be fellows cycling out from Mullingar to Crookedwood and from other places as well.

My mother came from Multifarnham, from the townland of Ballinreddra, from a farming background of similar size farm, which bordered the shores of Lough Derravaragh. We went on our summer holidays every year to our grandparents. I remember my grandparents very well. It was a real treat to visit them. They lived in a long thatched house and my uncles lived there, my two uncles, Uncle Tom and Jack. They didn't marry till late in life, well into their 30's. Girls married younger. My mother had a younger sister Rose, she worked at home with her mother, but she died young, at a young age, when she was only thirty-five.

A farmer at that time was a man that had so many acres of tillage, he'd have so many acres of grassland, he'd have so many milch cows sufficient to rear a family on, and stock for sale occasionally. He'd be tilling a fair amount and have a cross variety of vegetables. At that time a farm had to be self-supporting and to support a family. That's what a farm was doing, supporting a family. I suppose we had about eighty acres, ninety acres.

---

[4] 56 pounds or a half a hundred weight is equal to 25.4 kilos.

THE HOUSE AT HOME

My family were considered reasonable size farmers, I suppose. They were considered to be the farmers of the area. The Lovelys and Rourkes, who had a two-roomed cottage, were tenants on the land, and I think there was another small house. They all lived off it, the estate fed them and they all worked on the farm and got a few shillings. I had the impression as a child that everyone was so happy, come day go day.

In the house at home we had a kitchen, the dairy – a little room off the kitchen, and the parlour. When you came in the door into the hall, the kitchen was on your right, the parlour on your left and straight ahead was the stairs to the bedrooms. The parlour was the special room you brought people to, for different occasions and for family occasions. It was always a treat to eat in the parlour, at festivities or the like of that. We'd be in the parlour all over the Christmas time, at Easter too. It was like a sitting room. It was also the room Mother would take someone to if she wanted a private chat, rather than sitting at the table in the kitchen.

There were three bedrooms. There was 'the big bedroom', a big double room that had a fireplace and extended the front of the house over the parlour. There were four double beds in the big bedroom over the parlour. We'd sleep two in a bed but on a cold night we might sleep top and tails. Whoever was in first could choose top or tail. When we were small we could sleep four to a bed, lengthways or across. My parents slept in the bedroom above the fireplace over the kitchen. The third bedroom had a window that looked out over the garden. The rooms were very large and there was loads of room for more beds if we wanted to put them in. We had iron posted beds as well as wooden ones.

Granny Lynam, she lived with us, a little woman with a shawl. I don't know where she sat in the house. I just remember her being around.

We had no electricity growing up, we had candles and we had paraffin oil. We had a lamp up on the wall with a globe on it, and that was the light in the kitchen. The light upstairs would have been something similar; it was a candle carried round on a candlestick. What would I compare it to? It was like an enamel saucer with a centre in it where you would stand the candle and there was a loop on the side that you would hold with your finger, you would hold it there and carry it around. Half a candle was better that a full new candle 'cause you would always be watching for the balance of the light. You would use that to go up the stairs and then you would leave it on the table in the room. The candlestick was very safe; there was no grease, because it collected all the grease that would fall off the top of the candle.

We would have lamps where we needed them. Sometimes in winter there was an oil lamp on the top of the landing. The framed picture of the Sacred Heart with the lamp burning underneath was hanging on the kitchen wall. The Sacred Heart lamp was always burning, the little lamp with the little red globe or a white globe whatever the case might be. It would be fed by a wick to some oil and it burned away. That would be lighting permanently.

On wild windy nights in the wintertime you could always say, "Before the night is out we will see Mrs Lovely." Mrs Lovely was a very nice person, an elderly lady, she always wore a bonnet. She lived alone in a cottage on the land where she had reared all her children. She was very frightened of the wind, the noise of the wind, and on very windy nights she would make her way down to us and stay with us the night and go home the following morning.

The house was fairly well heated by the big fire in the open hearth[5] in the kitchen, where my mother did all the cooking and the baking. Mother did all the cooking and baking on the open fire. There were metal kettles and cooking pots, which you hung on the crane.[6] For baking there were different sized cast iron pot ovens, with legs.

When Mother was going to bake she would put on a good fire so that the coals and grisha would get red-hot. These coals were put under the pot oven, which would be off the floor on its little four legs, and the cast iron lid of the oven would be covered in hot coals or grisha. What we called 'grisha', I think it is an Irish word, was little bits of burning black turf, not the spongy turf. The turf had to be good quality for grisha so that it would keep hot and do the job. When bread was made it was left outside to cool.

You could sit into the hearth on the hob. In our hearth at home, like in most hearths, there was a space under the hob where you could sweep in the ashes. Early in the morning, my

---

[5] The hearth was under the chimney of the house where the open fire was made. There were built-in stone benches inside in the hearth on either side of the open fire where you could sit in and toast yourself, this was the hob. "As hard as the hob of hell" was an expression often used by Treasa. People always used cushions on the hob to soften their seat.

[6] The crane was an iron bar that crossed the hearth and had a crooked/hooked bar hanging from it on which you hung the pots over the fire. It was on a swivel so that you could swing it out in front and remove pots in safety.

mother would take the ashes out in a bucket and put them down in the ash pit down in the field or in a gripe.[7]

You would do your exercise[8] in the room off the kitchen or in your bedroom upstairs where you would have a bit of privacy. If you felt cold you could come and get heat off the fire in the kitchen.

Keeping snug in bed in the winter time

At night-time, if it was cold, you got a hot bottle, or a jar. That would be put at the foot of your bed and you could play around with it and make sure you got your share of the bottle or the jar. The hot bottle, as we called it, was an ordinary bottle with a screw top, and filled up with hot water. The jar was a delph jar, oblong with a special bung or plug in the top of it. They would have originally been whiskey or spirit jars.

We had quilts for our beds for the winter. Every year when we would be plucking geese, all the feathers would be saved. According as you had a pillowslip full of feathers they would be put away and you would start on another pillowslip and you might have two pillowslips or four or five pillowslips of feathers, lovely soft feathers and they would make up a quilt. We had the ordinary blankets, from Foxford Woollen Mills of Mayo, that's what we had for our blankets. Our sheets were made from linen flour bags. We used to get flour by the four stone bag. On the one side would be *St. Patrick's of Liverpool, Genuine White Flour,* it was only a brand name, then there was another one *Goodbody's of Clara,* those were the flour mills. When you would get a bag of flour you would be particularly anxious that you wouldn't tear the bag because if you did, you'd have to stitch it again. Well, those bags were put to one side and when you had four bags there - I don't know how long it would take us to go through four four-stone bags of flour - they would be washed, washed in washing soda, or in whatever would take out all the colouring. When the colouring would be washed out, the four bags would be put and stitched together and that would make an everlasting sheet, because they were linen. And you could buy finer linen, less coarse, and that would make a second sheet.

You would often see a girl going to school with a flour sack. If you were to cut a hole in the bottom of a flour bag and put your head out through, well, that's what it was like it. And then there would always be a comment. "Did you see so and so with the new St. Patrick's flour bag on her back" or, "Oh she thinks she's great advertising St. Patrick's

---

[7] A gripe was a trench at the edge of a field and that was dug out to build up a ditch. You could sow a whitethorn on the ditch and that would become a hedge in time, a whitethorn hedge.

[8] Homework, given by the teachers at school.

flour on her back" No matter how hard and how often you washed out the cloth, it was very hard to wash out the print.

My mother did all the washing by hand. The garden at the back of the house was surrounded by a clipped hedge. Along the top bank my mother would spread and dry the big sheets, along the tops of the hedges. She would then starch and iron them. She used to rinse the sheets in 'Red Robin' starch and then they were ironed. They were crisp when they were ironed. My mother would put the metal iron in front of the fire; she'd put it on a rest to keep it clean and out of the ashes. There was another type of iron, it had a box or slot in the middle of it. The way that worked is that you'd put a piece of iron, right into the burning fire till it was red-hot. You would then take it out with the tongs, and put it into the box in the iron. I think they were called a box iron.

We had a pony and trap; we didn't have a car. As children we would walk everywhere. Aunt Bridie had a car. I remember well she often used to ask us "Which side of the road do I stay on when I go out?" because Marlinstown road, which wasn't a tarmacadam road, joined the main Dublin-Mullingar road about a half mile from our house. There were several houses along the Marlinstown road, but nothing at all like the numbers of houses today.

THE FARM AT HOME

The farmyard

The farmyard was just off the front of the house and there was a substantial amount of stables and all that. To the left of the house was the car shed and the milking parlour. The first thing you would see when you would come out the front door was the marvellous pump, about ten or fifteen yards away from the front door, where we used to pump the loveliest spring water, fresh water, very fresh water. It was an old fashioned pump, with a pump trough, a granite trough. It had to be cleaned out fresh each day, you'd clean out whatever vegetable or whatever may be left in the trough after anything and everything that would have been washed in the trough that day. The over-flow from the pump would be released out into a big dike into the fields at the back.

When I got older I used to wonder who were all the friends we had that were coming to our place. People would be coming to collect water, the weather would be very, very warm and they would be coming to our place with two big milk cans or a small barrel. Some people wouldn't have a pump or a well in their own place. They would come and help themselves to water from our pump. One would help the other, filling a milk churn full, or loading it onto a pony and trap, or an ass and cart, or whatever. Naturally we knew all the people from all around; they would be our neighbours. Our pump was never dry; there was always water.

The yard had a sandy surface, but it was cobble-stoned in front of the house. The yard and the buildings were always kept very clean. There was a time and a place for everything. Once winter had come and gone, anywhere or anything that needed to be touched up was done and painted. The carts and whatever else had all to be painted too.

But the big job, it was the one thing my mother insisted upon, was the whitewashing. It was an annual thing. The house and farm buildings were whitewashed every year, at a certain time. Mother would do it herself, but she would also ask us to help. I was doing the whitewashing when I was eight years old. We would go over and get the lime from the man across the canal line - Horans. They would burn the lime. There, across there along the canal line, it was full of holes and hollows. The bank was all dug out with spades and shovels to get out the lumps of stone. They would burn the stone then, and bring out the lime.

When my mother got the lime, she would get blue ball[9] and she would boil up the lime with water. When the lime was bubbling, really bubbling, she would put in the blue ball,

---

[9] Blue ball, came as a blue lump and was a whitening agent.

and next thing you would have the whitewash ready to paint the walls. In Mother's place in Ballinreddra - I'm sure they still have it the same way- the yard would be as clean and neat, it would be neat and complete. Grandfather Loughrey, Mother's father, he would be really exact. I don't think Granny Loughrey would be that interested, though maybe she would, well, I suppose they leaned off each other ... You would walk into the place and you would say "My God" and then you would go up to Marlinstown and you would find that Mother had done the same thing up there, till it got beyond her.

The buildings were painted with black tar, which gave a lovely touch to the white wash that had been done. We all had to do our bit, even though we might have had someone in to help out. My mother was very particular about the black border around the base of the freshly whitewashed buildings. You would go along all the walls of the buildings and mark them off about a foot and a half off the ground with this tar. The tar would be glistening. I don't know what type of tar it was. It was customary to see the black along the base of the wall. Well, that was Mother!

And then there was the garden... we will come to that later.

Keeping animals

You always kept a few pigs, you'd always have one extra that you'd sell, and you'd be selling a pig now and again. It was as easy to keep two as one. If you had a pig killed, well, that kept you going with three meals a day, breakfast in the morning, midday meal and whatever in the evening. And you'd have hens and chickens and stock all around the yard. If you had a good few eggs you'd sell them off. The butter was always – well, everything we ate was produced on the farm. We would keep about ten or twelve geese in the yard and we kept turkeys later on when they became popular. But we had bronze turkeys; we didn't have white turkeys. The only difference was in the feathers; there wasn't a difference in the taste. Before turkeys came into popularity, we always had goose for Christmas.

We had labourers working on the farm at certain times of the year, we probably had one man working for us all year round and of course when we got big enough it wasn't necessary. There wouldn't be farm workers in continuity. There would be a local man who was a farm labourer, he was like one of the house, and he'd live a short distance away. He'd ask for permission to put down a drill of potatoes for himself, and you'd put in about three drills of about a hundred yards long. There'd be no such thing as short drills of fifty yards or so. He'd get a drill of potatoes or two for himself and he'd get at them at his own leisure, therefore he'd have potatoes. Apart from whatever money he was getting, he'd be getting the milk off the farm as well, and whatever else would be produced off the farm.

The garden at the back of the house, with the clipped hedge all around, was used for sowing kitchen vegetables. About half an acre was taken up in garden, this was only for small vegetables, like carrots, cabbage, onions, and beetroot. The orchard had plums and damsons and pear and apple trees growing down both sides. You'd have turnips out the field for pig feed, you'd have parsnips out the field, you'd have field carrots, you know the big ones with clay on them, you still see them in the country markets. The only thing you'd have to buy was the tea and the sugar.

Growing up with cows and daily milking

As you came into the yard from the road and looked down to the door of the house the dairy was the first building on the right. When we started the delivery of milk to Mullingar, when we started the Dairy, that is where we prepared the milk for the churns for delivery to the town. That's where the milk would congregate and be put on benches, down in the dairy, after the milking. The milk would be left there.

It was different earlier on, when I was younger. Going back a bit in time, to when I was five or eight years of age and before we had the Dairy, we had six to eight cows that we would be milking. My mother did the milking by hand. You might be asked to go up and give her a hand in the milking parlour. For every cow you'd milk she would milk two.

Did you ever hear the song about the milking?

> *"And as she sat down most homely for the milking of her cow...*
The girl's father was recommending to her to get married.
> *"Oh daughter dearest daughter whatever will you do"*
And the song goes on
> *"Well, if I do get married, I'll do the same as Ma and you,*
> *I'll be mistress of my dairy, my buttermilk and my cow*
> *And my husband too I bet you, for the humour is on me now".*

After milking, some milk would be put aside for drinking as fresh milk. Some would be used for feeding young calves. At that time I'd say there might be ten to twelve calves and then they could be buying a few extra calves. They would all be fed off the milk or buttermilk, whatever there would be there. Then there was the milk put aside for making butter, that milk was taken into the house, into what we called the dairy. It was a little room off the kitchen and the milk was kept in crocks there. The crocks were delph crocks; you'd still see some of them around today. It would be kept there till it went thick, I wouldn't say sour, or until my mother was ready to churn.

Making the butter

When there would be sufficient milk put away, it would be churned and the butter made. Butter would be made at least once a week and of course my mother made the butter. Generally milk for making butter would be left standing in the crocks for a week, sometimes up to two weeks, till it was thick milk. Then it was put in the churn. We had an end-over-end churn,[10] I suppose it would hold about three or four gallons of milk. The end-over-end churn was put up on a stand. There was a handle on the side of the churn to turn it over and you turned the churn end-over-end, end-over-end. The lid, it was screwed down onto a rubber or 'bussions'[11] and there was a little bit of glass that you could see through. This allowed you to check the stage of the turning of the milk. You would first see little lumps of milk, milk would go like it was sour, then you would see little lumps of butter forming. You would see little yellow specks and the more you would churn it the bigger the yellow specks got.

It would take over an hour turning the churn, end-over-end, end-over-end. You would get about three or four pounds weight of butter off that amount of milk, though I wouldn't be really certain of the weight. The butter was taken out of the churn then, and put into a wooden utensil, that was always spotlessly clean, what we called a 'keeler'. It was like a round container, made of oak, I know that much. It was always scrubbed out and scalded out with boiling water. My mother would mix the big lump of butter with her hands to get all the milk out of the butter, and it would be rinsed with cold water and rinsed and rinsed again, till finally there was nothing left only all butter.

Naturally, it was farmer's butter and it would be salty. A fair amount of salt would be added to the butter, to preserve it. Some people liked a milder flavour though the butter would be completely tasteless without the salt. Butter patens, or spades would be used to cut up the squares of butter, like a cut of cheese, and to shape the butter.

There was always butter enough for home and extra to sell to the shop or in the market. The butter would be put in greaseproof paper and wrapped up. You would then take it to

---

[10] The end-over-end churn was shaped like a wooden barrel and it was mounted on a wooden cradle. The operation of a hand crank caused the barrel to revolve end-over-end.

[11] bussions was the seal that helped to tightly secure the lid.

the market or to the shops; they would all be looking for butter. The quality of your butter decided if you got a good price for it or not. Some people's butter, they would say, would have a taste off it after a few days, and you wouldn't use it. But Mrs Lynam's butter, my mother's, was always looked for. I'm not just saying that 'cause she was my mother, but she was very particular. When you would buy goods in the shop they would deduct a certain amount of money as their payment for the butter.

If we had a lot of milk every day, if we had a lot of cows milking at the time, we would be filling four crocks of milk every day from the milking, and adding four more crocks of milk to the stock in the dairy. My mother would then reduce what we called the 'thick milk' in the crock. She would cut a slice off the top of the crock of thick milk, with a saucer. The milk would have thickened over the week or two; it would be like the consistency of custard and thick enough to take a slice off it. That milk would be fairly concentrated and what she would do is put a small amount of thick milk into a small churn, and that would be churned instead of a full end-over-end churn. When you churned this small amount of milk, the result would be that there would be less buttermilk and more butter. All the butter would come to the top in less time.

Butter would be made about once a week and of course my mother made the butter. But we used to use a lot of the butter at home. We used it at every meal. On Fridays you would probably use more butter than on other days. At that time working men out on the farm would come in on a Friday and they would get about six ounces[12] of butter on their plate with lovely floury potatoes. They would also get a mug of buttermilk and they had that. If they had a wish for a cup of tea after, they would have that too. Other men wouldn't take tea.

That would be their Friday dinner. Well, everyone fasted[13] at that time on a Friday, fasting was very much observed in the country at that time. You wouldn't be going in to Mullingar for fish. If there happened to be a bit of fish, you could have it, but you wouldn't really get anything except that red fish, cod fish, that smoked fish. And the fellas wouldn't relish that. They would be so happy, including myself, with the floury potatoes and the butter and the buttermilk, though me personally, I preferred, not the buttermilk but, the fresh milk. I was never a lover of buttermilk. Buttermilk was the liquid that was left in the churn after the butter making, when the big lump of butter was removed from the churn.

---

[12] Six ounces is 170.1 grams.
[13] Friday was a day of total abstinence from meat.

Cutting our turf

We had a turf bank in the local bog at Baltrasna, alongside the railway. It would have been about a mile to the turf bank. There was another bog at Curraghmore. We had a high bank and a low bank. You would have to strip the top of the bog on the high bank every year by cutting down two to three feet first, to take off the top of the bog. What you would take off the top of the high bank, you would throw down on the low bank where you would have cut the turf the year before. You would level it out and make it possible to dry turf on the lower bank.

So you would work at the high bank. When you had stripped the bank of the topsoil, you would start cutting off sods of turf. At this level you would begin to get brown turf. It would be no good for heat but it was good for starting a fire, it was fast burning. Then you would go down to the black - that was the best turf. In some part of the bog you get a good mix of black and brown. The black would be very heavy and soggy, but it would dry out black.

We always used the wing sleán. You would give it a bit of a twist or a screw to loosen the sod of turf that you had just cut. You'd slide the sod off the sleán by throwing it to another fella who would put it into the bog barrow. The bog barrow was like a wheelbarrow. A load would be wheeled about thirty yards away and emptied, making a pile of about twenty sods of turf. These piles were left at a distance to each other. When the turf was sufficiently dry to move, you would separate the sods and spread them out to dry until they were dry enough to handle. Then you would put them in bigger heaps what we called 'clamps' or 'grugs'. When they were really dry, you would bring them home with a horse and cart or with creels or crates and you would stack them in the turf shed.

In some parts of the bog we would get to cut eight to nine feet of turf, a mix of black and brown. If you went below the black, you would get to the gravel or 'lack' as we called it. There would be no more bog after that. The bog would grow again into wasteland or bogland. Mrs Smith owned the bog, I think. We paid rent to use the bog, but it always seemed that everyone owned the bog, because people worked on the bog together, at the same time of the year. In April or May you could start cutting turf, it depended though on when people were free.

Growing, treshing and selling corn

There would be neighbourly sales,[14] and you'd sell oats and potatoes. You wouldn't need all the oats you'd be growing or all the potatoes you'd be growing, you wouldn't need them all. Having a surplus depended on what you'd need for yourself and after you had sufficient for seed for the following year. Seed potatoes were always kept for sowing the following year.

The oats were threshed with a steam-threshing mill that came in every year and it was worked there in the haggard.[15] There would be two men up feeding the mill, the sheaves would be cut, shaken out a bit and the men would feed the oats into the mill, head first. The straw would be kicked out the tail end of the mill and the oats would kick out at the top end, filling about three sacks at a time. The straw, lovely sweet golden straw would be saved for thatching and for bedding for the animals. The sacks of oats were always referred to as barrels of oats. On the day of the thrashing you would have so many barrels of oats or wheat as the case might be. Some of the oats would be sent to the Thomastown mill in Killucan for milling and to be turned into meal, the rest of the oats you would be selling. Some of the oats would be cracked out, or as we'd say, manufactured at the mill, we'd refer to it as cracked oats, it would be sufficient for feeding the stock.

We sold our own wheat and we never bought oatmeal, that's for sure. There was no such thing in our time as flakemeal. I remember well you would bring the wheat to the mill in Thomastown beyond Killucan. If you waited you could have the wheat ground. You would get back coarse wheaten meal. If my mother was baking she would put in a handful of that St Patrick's Liverpool flour and that would make it a little less coarse than the pure wheaten meal bread.

---

[14] Big farmers would be selling to the big market. Neighbourly sales were between neighbours, it allowed a neighbour to buy a small quantity of produce from another neighbour that you knew had over and above what they needed and produced for their own family.

[15] The haggard, was a small field or a partitioned corner of a field near the house where the work was done.

Summer 1925. (L-R) Tom (6), Pat (8), Father, Bill (4), Rose (18 months), Mother
Jim (nearly 3), Josie. Still to join the family were Mary and Teresa.

This is an old photograph of the school children of the Curraghmore N.S., taken about 50 years ago, and below is a list of the names of the pupils. I am sure it will bring back memories long forgotten of faces of earlier years. The photograph itself was sent in by Mrs. Molly Corcoran, Belmont, Mullingar, formerly Molly Flynn and she herself is one of the pupils.

Top row, left to right, Jimmy Quirke, Pat Coffey, Tom Lynam, Willie Lynam, Johnny McCormack, Jimmy O'Neill, Frank Kiernan, Pat Lynam. Second row, Moira Fullam, Rosie Mee, Kathleen McCormack, Delia Shaw, Annie Dalton, Maggie Corroon, Katie Shaw, Nellie McCormack, Maggie O'Neill, Fannie Reilly. Third row, Lizzie Leonard, Liz Dalton, Mary Langan, Lizzie Langan, Aloque Dalton, Loreto McDonagh, Massie Dalton, Dee Reilly, Una Duignam, Lily Flynn, Lizzie Corroon, Molly Flynn, Babs Reilly, Alice Quirke. Fourth row, Nannie Langan, Christina Quirke, Bridie Conlon, Aggie Owens, Aileen McDonagh, Rosie Reilly, Thomas O'Neill, Joe Molloy, Dermot McDonagh, Tom Coffey, Tommie McDonagh, John Corroon. Fifth row, Christy Corroon, Nicky Langan, Anthony Fulham, Cyril Fulham, Matthew Coffey, Christy Dalton, John Flynn, Jimmy Lynam.

Photo courtesy of Molly Flynn. Printed in the Westmeath Examiner in the 1970's. Photographer unknown.

CHILDHOOD

Starting school

I started school at five. I remember my first day at school. I got on very, very well at school and the second day I got on extremely well. The big story of my second day at school was that when I went home, and they asked me how I had got on, I told them I had a marvellous day "I am now in second class". The first day I was in first class, I was put in the front bench. The second day they put me in the second bench, so I was in the second class.

We went to school through the fields, I suppose the best part of two and a half miles, jumping the drains and jumping over or running through the bit of a bog. We used to take off our boots and hide them under a hedge somewhere, in a place where we would find them when we were coming home. We could run faster without boots. You could also be jeered if you were wearing shoes. I remember one of the days the priest called and we were sitting on the bank outside the school. And he looked at us and counted up "One, two, three" and made a remark jeering and looking to the one who was wearing shoes. "Why are you not like the rest, why are you wearing shoes?"

In the wintertime when the weather was really bad we had to go by the road, I don't think we were ever left to school. But we were able to shorten the road by being able to go through the fields.

We'd set off to school at nine o'clock in the morning; it would take three quarters of an hour. And it would take a half an hour to come home in the evening. For breakfast we had stir-about porridge from our own oats, plenty of fresh milk and homemade bread. We used to put salt on the porridge. It wasn't till I came to Dublin that I started to put sugar on it. If it was a cold morning we would have a rasher and an egg.

We brought lunch with us, always homemade bread, maybe two slices and milk in a lemonade bottle. Or if my father or my mother happened to be in town on a market day, they'd possibly bring home some white bread, 'loaf bread' as we'd refer to it, and we'd surely get this loaf bread, which was lovely to eat. It was a variety for the next day after them being at the market. I know that it would be twelve o'clock when you'd eat your lunch, but you'd be absolutely wall-falling with the hunger by the time you'd get home from school, after eating the white bread from Mullingar. There was no nourishment whatsoever in the loaf bread, no sustenance. I know it was lovely, but that was the one thing: how long could you last on it?

We'd surely be home by a quarter to four. We always rushed home; there was always three or four of us. Bill and Jim and I would be coming home together. Bill was never very fast, but Jim was a flyer and you couldn't keep up with him. He'd always be head and shoulders down. We would meet Jim as we came in home and he going out into the yard to do his jobs, his dinner over. We tried to trip him up one evening by tying and knotting a few fistfuls of rushes together, but it didn't work.

Your dinner would be on the table at four o'clock. You'd always have plenty of vegetables and potatoes and bacon. Monday you'd have bacon and cabbage, Tuesday you'd have cabbage and bacon. We had chicken and fowl, anything. We were very well fed and we were never short of farm butter. I was never really fond of buttermilk, but I loved fresh milk. There were people who'd give anything for a mug of buttermilk, especially if they were thirsty.

Doing our jobs

I often came home and you'd go down the fields and all you could see from here to eternity were potato drills or turnips to be weeded. It was wicked.

Other jobs that you'd do, well, you could be cleaning out stables. Cows and calves would have been in stables. You might have to yoke the pony and bring the stable manure from wherever it was, outside the stables, or the stable gate, and then bring it down to the manure heap and put it there. It was left there until such time as it was taken down to be put in the ground for the tillage.

We'd often have to pump water for the cattle in the wooden-gate field; there would be so many head of cattle in it. And we would have to pump the water for the cattle. We would pump fifty gallons of water into the big metal boiler, a bowl-shaped metal container. We pumped the water from the well below; there was always loads of water in the well below. As kids you'd be sick and tired of pumping water and you would take turns. As the cattle would come up to drink it, you, you'd whoosh them away. When we were nearly finished we would try to spray water over the top of the boiler, so that people would think we had done the job properly. I suppose we were trying to give the impression that we really did such a good job filling the boiler to the brim that it spilled over the top of the boiler. Later on, after my father died, and the Loughreys brought their cattle up from Ballinreddra to graze them in our big fields across the road, we had to pump a lot of water for the herds. Uncle Jack and Uncle Tom used to sell their cattle from our place in Marlinstown. I remember as kids, two of us, myself and Bill, or myself and Jim, used to drive the cattle into the Market Square in Mullingar where my uncles then sold them. We would have been nine and ten and twelve at the time. I drove the cattle on my own too, walking behind them.

There is one particular job that I remember. It's one job that sticks out when I think of it, and I ask myself "Why did I do this job?" and "What age was I when I did it?" We had the canal fields over by the canal; one particular field was full of tillage. There were turnips in it, there were potatoes in it. I remember well, it was in tillage for two or three years. At one end of the drill there was oats in it, and the turnips were in the other end of the field. And I remember there was a wall up around the canal side, at the bank side, and it was broken down. There were big stones that had fallen down and there was a load of dirt on top of them. I remember going over there one day, on a Saturday, and hearing my father saying "That wall is getting worse and some day you'll be able to build it up." I must have been about eight, or only nine at the time. I remember going over one Saturday and building up that wall, taking all the dirt away and building up those big stones. I remember putting in thin scraw[16] in between the stones and doing a nice job building up the wall. And I remember my father coming and giving me great credit for building up this wall and I so young.

In the wintertime I remember going down to Brennans beyond Baltrasna close to the railway track to bring them milk. The water would rise to such an extent on parts of that land that it might be difficult for the Brennans to get in and out. Pat and I would be sent down with a can of milk and to make sure that they were alright. You would normally cross the drain on a plank, but it became a river with the flood and you'd have to be really careful crossing then. It was awkward and you had to cross with great care. The Ledwiths lived close to the canal bridge. They used to go to Mullingar by ass and cart. On the way in and out of town, Maggie used to pull in and rest the ass at the corner near the end of the road. The ass was called Nancy. That's how the corner became known as Nancy's corner.

Going on errands into Mullingar

You might be sent into Mullingar on an errand. It was about three or four miles into the town. I remember once, God it just shows how young I was, I was sent in and told to leave a pair of shoes into the cobbler. I had only one thing in mind. In the middle of the town at the bend of the road, there was a shop called Loftus, a shoe shop. I remember seeing people leaving in shoes there, one time when I was in the town with my mother. So since I left home on the errand to bring the shoes to the cobbler, I had one thing in my mind and

---

[16]This was a thin slice of grass and clay from within the field. It would help bind the rock together and there was sufficient seed held within the grass and clay that in time would grow in and around the stones and therefore keep the wall always tightly in place.

that was to bring the shoes into Loftus', not up to Jack Deignan the cobbler, where my mother or father always brought the shoes. Of course I never thought of bringing the shoes up to Jack Deignan's. I should have remembered this, but Loftus' was the one that I knew. Well, someone went into Deignan's on the following Saturday evening to get the shoes, the Sunday shoes, and discovered that Deignan hadn't got them. The only way that they could discover where the shoes had been left was to go back out home, and not to talk to me, but to bring me back into Mullingar, to show them where I had left the shoes.

If I had to go to town to do an errand, I'd sometimes go in to Mary Martin in Mullingar, she lived in the thatched house at the Dublin Bridge and I'd get ten sweets for a penny and it would shorten the road on the way home. I'd tell myself that I'd have two sweets between the bridge and the pond outside the town, I'd have two more after that and I'd walk very fast to the next stop, where I'd have two more sweets. I'd have eight sweets eaten by the time I got home. That way I was able to shorten the road.

As children growing up, we made our own fun, whatever that may have been

You could be at anything, climbing, running, you could be up to anything. I was a bit of a tease. I remember one day I must have annoyed Mick Ryan, Lord have mercy on him, he was working out in the fields and I was messing about, I can't really remember what I really did to annoy him. Well, I annoyed him anyway and well, he caught me, and bundled me under his arm, carried me over to where the goat was tethered and what did he do? Well, didn't he milk the goat into my face. I was full of it.

There was a bit of a tease in Jim too; well, maybe he was more a daredevil. I remember coming home from mass on the pony and trap and Jim would cycle behind, I'd say he was only about eight. Well, every time we'd come to a part of the road where there were no bumps, he would take his hands off the handlebars. My poor mother would get so anxious. If she only knew the half of it. I remember out on the main road he used to wait till the bus was really up close, and then he'd dash out and fly across the road. He was always a flyer and so fast, but he'd put the heart crossways in you.

I remember once teasing with Josie in the house, I think my parents were away, maybe my parents were out. She really got annoyed and chased me, maybe with the tea towel. Immediately outside the front door in Marlinstown were cobblestones, just in front of the pump in the yard that gave us the finest of spring water. Well, Josie was chasing me with the wet cloth, after I really annoying her. I turned so quickly and made one big chase to get away through the door. As I passed out through the door I made an even bigger chase, but I fell on my two knees and two legs and cut them. I cut one big gash in my knee, well, I cut

22

a lump out of the knee, and it was raw, with stones and gravel stuck in it. I had to sit down to take out all the stones and the gravel. It was awful. It took so long to get the gravel out of it, God I'll never forget it. It was bandaged up then. You can see still where the lump was taken out.

We all got knocks, Mary once nearly took a slice off her arm, they had to get the nailbrush to scrub the gravel and grit out of her arm, and there was no anaesthetic. Teresa once was sent to find help at the mill, to get one of the Ryans, we were short of help. Well, she ripped a cut down her leg with the pedal of the bike, with the spike; there was no rubber on it. The spike cut deeply, the cut was about a half-inch deep right down the length of her leg. The doctor had to be sent for, and she just lay there while he stitched away, no anaesthetic or painkiller or anything.

There was one time I was at home on my own and had the yard to myself. I wasn't a child; I must have been about thirteen. Pat and the rest of them were probably down making hay. The man that was working for us, he had a bicycle. He was a low size man. One of the jobs that he used to do for us was to drag or pull drains, he had a thing like a big rake with prongs on it, and when he'd be finished, all the reeds and the grass growing in the rivers or in the drains would be all pulled out. Well, he would be working down in 'the bottoms'- that was the low lying land, and there would be no want for him up around the house, that's what he'd be doing. His bicycle was in the car-shed, alongside the pony and trap. It was about two o'clock in the day. I knew that he wouldn't be coming back up for lunch that day 'cause he would be having his lunch, picnic style. Someone would bring him down his lunch to the fields. He wouldn't be coming up for his dinner till the evening, and I knew that he wouldn't be back until five o'clock. So I got out his bicycle and got up on it and cycled up the yard. It was great stuff, I was delighted.

When you get up the yard at home, you come out through a gate. Well, I hit the spud stone between the gates and I stumbled a bit. On each side of the avenue outside the gate there was a ditch, or a gripe as you might call it, it was up about two feet higher than the road. Well, I lost control of the bicycle and I went straight into the ditch. The ditch was full of rocks and all sorts of things and covered in nettles. I could see nothing of the stuff only the nettles, I thought "Sacred heart" and I was determined that I wasn't going to let them get near my face. But God, I made for the wall on the far side. But by that time, I wasn't scalded, but roasted with nettles and I was well cut too. I went down home and put a bit of a bandage on it, I remember putting something on it, I'm not really sure what, 'cause the nettle stings were something shocking, God I remember it well, I would have had short trousers on. It was really terrible.

Well, I was going for the cows that evening; they had to be milked. I'd usually get the cows at about three o'clock in the evening, milk them and get ready to go to town. You'd go to town with a big churn of milk in the pony and trap. That would be the routine anyway. The churn would have a tap on it, it was easier then, and you could easily fill the delivery can for delivering the milk. Anyway by the time I was going for the cows, the pain of the nettles was settling down, and I had begun to feel the pain of the gash in the ankle that I had made with the fall on the stones. Well, when I went to pull down my top-stocking to find out what the leg was like, I saw that the purple long stocking was stuck into the wound with the blood from the cut. There was a right gash in the shin and the pain was something else. It was a summer's evening, and there had been a big shower of rain. In the field there were fresh puddles filled with clear rainwater. I went over to one of them; it was like a little pond between two pucáns.[17] I washed and washed the leg until I finally got the stocking unstuck out of the wound. I took off the stocking and I used it to wash the wound clean with the water out of the puddle in the field.

Well, my leg pained me all that night, and the next morning it was worse. It swelled all round, it swelled up to my knee; it swelled up to my thigh. It was all swelled up. I was told to put my leg up on something, to keep my heel up higher than my knee. I was told not to leave where I was sitting, someone else would do my jobs. Well, I put up with that for I think six weeks.

I couldn't very well say that I was after taking your man's bike out of the car-shed, and going up the yard and having a great spin on it and it all gas. They would have had sympathy for me if I told them the truth. But I didn't. I told them that I was getting out of the pony and trap and that I banged my shin off the step at the back of the trap. And that lived on as the terrible story of Tom banging his shin off the step of the trap, and how he didn't look after it with the stocking stuck in it. They made out that it was a big story, though I can tell you, it was even a bigger story than they ever made out. Even the knuckles in my knee were all swollen out, though the big cut was down at the shin. After about six weeks it eased, maybe in a little less time, but I wasn't able to do anything for six weeks. The blood poisoning was so great – its a living memory, I can feel the pain still. It wasn't until years after that I finally told the truth of what really happened.

Saying the prayers

I can safely say that from the time that I could say the 'Our Father' or the 'Hail Mary' that I was included in the family rosary. Saying the rosary was an absolute must. The beads were left over on the dresser and you would each have your own little beads or big beads.

---

[17] Pucáns were clumps of rushes or reeds that would grow, even on well-grazed land.

When it was time for the rosary you'd be handed over your beads by whoever was nearest the dresser and you'd kneel down on the floor. In my father's day - and we carried on the tradition - my father would give out the five decades of the rosary, my mother would give out the litany of the Blessed Virgin, she would know it off by heart, and after that there would be a couple, a few, ejaculations. And if there was anything special, it would be mentioned in the course of the rosary, we would remember a neighbour who might be ill, or someone sick in hospital or pray for the success of someone who might have gone away.

And then each one would say their decade of the rosary, if they were able. If there weren't enough of us able for the five decades, someone might start off a decade and another might finish off the other half-decade, or say a second one. And according as you got that bit older, or able to answer, you could say a decade on your own. Like it carried on in my own family. I don't know which of my own family, which one of you, when you were away doing your own thing, wrote in a letter "There's one thing I want to find out now, who is saying my decade when I am not there?". That is as clear to me today as it was then. I'd love to be able to say who is saying the decade, but unfortunately, like the rest of the world, people are slipping up, but it goes on and on and on in places where people are starting up a family. I remember well giving the advice to someone in my own family, I think it was Bill, when he was getting married. I sent him a picture of Our Lady saying, "If you are true to Our Lady, Our Lady will be true to you". And I really meant it.

Making music, picking up tunes and the gramophone at home

I never bought sweets, I'd save up any money I'd get, and buy something. A trump was the cheapest thing you could buy – a Jews' harp was the proper name for it. I bought several of them. I'd buy a mouth organ if I had the price of it; I'd do without the sweets. The way I learned the tunes... well, they would just come to you. You'd just pick them up. 'Miss McCloud', well, that was a popular tune; you'd hear people whistle it and you'd just pick it up. My mother didn't sing, my father would lilt an ould 'come-all-ye' What's that one Conor sings now?... 'The Galway Shawl', my father would lilt that. My mother liked music, she liked all the ould 'come-all-ye's. She was forever buying records. We had a gramophone at home. She would have all the songs you could ever hear. She loved listening to them; she had all of them written down in a big book. I'd pick up the airs of the songs.

Uncle Tom and Uncle Jack both played the melodeon, not the accordion. I heard my Uncle Jack say once, that if he was at the fair and he heard a particular artist or those wandering musicians, he would always listen to their tunes. He told me that one day he followed a fellow whistling a tune and followed him till he had the tune. When he went home, he took down the melodeon, and he tried to play the tune. He was able to play it by the following day because he'd picked up the air listening while following your man home. Granny, Lord of mercy on her, would often say that Uncle Tom was better at the melodeon than Uncle Jack, but sure Uncle Jack came after him, and it was easier for him to just take it up.

My mother loved flowers

My mother was very interested in flowers, really very interested. She was a life long member of Rowans. Rowans used to send her out the catalogue every spring. She would go through the catalogue to see the flowers and to pick the ones she liked, and she'd try them out. I often told you before how she tried out the lupines. She saw the lupines in the catalogue and she thought they would go nice, and had put the lupines up at the top of the garden, where all the sweet pea grew.

I remember my mother was ill at that time, I'm not sure why, but she was ill in bed. I told her about the thing she had sowed. At that time, after the milking I'd do the garden, trim the hedges, and get rid of any bits of grass that would be growing along the walls. She called me up after breakfast one morning and said "Tom will you ever bring me up the lupine out of the garden? I would dearly love to see what it turned out like, 'cause I was particularly anxious when I bought the seeds that time as to what way it would turn out". She wanted me to cut it so that she could see it in bloom.

I can remember it well, going out the garden gate and going down the garden. I can tell you exactly where I got it. I can still see it now, exactly where the lupines were growing, though the garden is now a field. I cut that lupine to bring it up to her. I always remember it so well 'cause it had a peppermint smell. And I brought that in the garden gate, and brought it up to her in the room. That was Mother's room over the kitchen fire. I brought it over to her in the bed, in her feather bed. We always had the ordinary ticks[18] but Mother had this wonderful, this height of feathers, a feather bed, and you could build it up to a terrific height.

I well remember a night many years later in that same room. Tom McSweeney and I had cycled from Galway and we got into the house in Marlinstown, it was nearly half past twelve at night, they were waiting for us at the house. I remember it rang twelve o'clock at the Dublin Bridge and we still had to go in to Marlinstown. When we finally arrived McSweeney fell down and I asked what was wrong with him. "Lynam" says he "I'm too hungry to eat and I'm too tired to sleep" and he went upstairs and into the bed "Lynam come up here" he shouted down, and I went up and found him. And he was lost, sunk

---

[18] Ticks were a heavy stuffed mattress for the bed.

down in the feathers. I can still see all that, where the furniture was and all that. The two of us slept in that big bed that night.

The Royal Canal

The canal starts near East Wall in Dublin you can see it there at Binn's Bridge or at Cross Guns Bridge and it comes down along through Mullingar. I remember barges on the canal drawn by horses. I could show you the marks of the ropes that would have cut into the bridge from the rubbing against the bridge as they went through, bringing the beer to Mullingar.

There was a toss school up near the Canal Bridge, Baltrasna Bridge. In the summer kids would swim in the canal. I remember we used to go up to watch Peter Moore dive off the top of Baltrasna Bridge down into six foot of water below. We used to walk across the top of the bridge, if my mother knew she would be very frightened. I remember being there on the occasion that Phil Purcell, a vet, swam from Saunder's Bridge to Baltrasna Bridge. When he came out of the water he wasn't able to stand up; it took him a few minutes to come round.

I never really learned to swim. I never did swim, I never could swim. Not like Niamh and Bianca, well, they are just fantastic, and Meave well, she.... I have never seen any child enjoy the water so much. All of my grandchildren are great swimmers, but I never did swim. I remember once trying to swim during the very warm weather. We got a long rope, a harness rope, and we went up to try to swim under Baltrasna Bridge. The way we tried to swim was, well, we got the long harness rope, and we tied a big loop at the end of it. Someone would go over the other side of the canal and throw you over the rope. You'd put it over our head and under your arms and walk into the canal as far as you could under the Baltrasna Bridge, the canal was narrower at the bridge and we thought it was a bit more shallow. Then you'd hold on to the rope and the person on the far side would pull you over the rest of the way. God help us and we thought we were swimming. One day Matty Murtagh decided he'd have a go. But he'd only trust Jim to pull him across on the harness rope. Well, instead of walking into the canal like the rest, Matty made a big lunge and landed half way into the canal, driving water over the canal bank. He went right down under. Poor Jim, there was so much slack on the rope he couldn't pull the rope fast enough. First he had to pull Matty up, and then over and out of the water. When I think of it!

We used to dip the sheep in the canal. Sheep are one animal that really hate water. We would put them in, one by one, tied to a rope and then with a big long stick, poke at their coats swishing the wool around in the water as best we could. Of course you would only do this job in fine weather and on a really good sunny day. Well, the difference in their coats when they would dry out. Their wool was so white compared to before the wash. We always used to do that job before they were shorn, but the sheep never liked it.

Picnics

Sometimes my mother would bring us over to the canal bank for a picnic. The wooden-gate field was a great field for hay. On a Sunday afternoon or evening at hay making time, my mother would often say, "I think we'll have a picnic this evening", and she would prepare the tea. We'd have a fine big homemade current cake and whatever else, and she would bring it all out to the hayfield. We'd all be playing and fooling around and whatever else and next thing we'd be called for tea and we'd have it at the butt of the cock of hay. After the tea, we'd all be off rambling around, and my mother and father would be talking about the hay and work and other things. Other times Mother might put a tart and some things in a basket and off we'd go. That might be done for a birthday.

In the summer time, we would all pack up and go on the pony and trap; you could pull in to a field or a lake and make a picnic out of it.

In the summer time too I remember the wild strawberries growing all along the bank on the road at Marlinstown, before you came to the first bend on the road. We used to pick them on Sunday coming home from mass. They would be growing along on the right bank of the road before you came to the 'cup and saucer'.[19] We went to the last mass on Sunday. In the fields beyond, we picked mushrooms.

My mother was great for making our clothes

My mother made all our clothes, short pants, shirts. My mother could make anything, and she had a sewing machine, a foot pedal sewing machine. It wasn't a Singer it was one like it. It was a Bedford sewing machine, made before Singer, but it would do the same job. She got a Singer later. She used to buy material and make every stitch. Mother would make shirts, everything you could possibly think of. As far as the sewing machine was concerned, she could do anything with it. She never served her time to it but she was brilliant. If you tore your coat or your pants she would put a patch on it and nobody could ever see where it went on, she did it so neatly. People in the country then, might say "Oh I don't know how to do that" but not my mother, she was very able. Naturally she would

---

[19] A cup and saucer was painted on each of the gateposts of the drive into the family house in Marlinstown. It was a symbol of welcome and to let everyone know that there was always a cup of tea if you were passing by. The house was always known as the 'Cup and Saucer' from Patrick Lynam's time in the 1860's, because of the topiary bush near the entrance.

never make very good clothes. She would buy a few yards of material, and make our clothes, not too coarse; she certainly made corduroy trousers. Velvet material was worn a lot. My mother would buy velvet material and make a velvet suit, no problem. As far as sewing on buttons is concerned, well, I suppose anyone could do that, but I don't manage it so well.

You'd be brought in to Mullingar for shoes, or maybe for Communion or Confirmation. For your Communion you went into Mullingar to TL Hutchinson, a Protestant, a lovely first class drapery store, on the corner of the Market Square. Every second person, coming up to the week before Confirmation, would be in getting their Confirmation clothes. The clothes were the very same as you would get today. There would be a suit for the Confirmation. You could have whatever style you wanted, but we were always dressed in a suit. There were no long trousers; we would have been in short trousers till we were ten or eleven years of age. I remember I had one of those little jackets, like what Conor would wear today, 'hook and eye' buttons up the front. There was nothing more special than your Communion or Confirmation. Your Communion or Confirmation clothes would be considered your best clothes and you would wear them for a couple of years till you would grow out of them, or till they were worn out.

Girls were dressed out to the nines in their long white lace. Lace dresses, lace over dresses, down to their ankles, like a wedding frock. There's no difference today in the occasion. If you saw children going to their First Holy Communion today, sure they would be dressed up costing a fortune, lace, gloves, head-dress, everything. Everyone was trying to out-do the other then too, some things haven't changed.

Making my Confirmation

Pat and I got Confirmation on the same day. By the time you came to Confirmation there was a lot expected of you regarding your knowledge of your religion. You would be in the special Confirmation class for a few months beforehand. That would be known by everybody. You had to do a special, thorough, study of what Confirmation was all about and bible studies. Confirmation was every three years; there was three years between one Confirmation and the next. When the Confirmation would be over, the Confirmation class would break up and you would go back to your different classes, whatever standard you were at the time. The Confirmation class was a very special class. The catechist would come round to the school for a period of time in that particular year, and there was a general build up of your religious knowledge. We often had to stay in at lunchtime or in the evenings. You made your Confirmation between ten and thirteen years of age. Some of the young ones were better than the older ones; some people were very good, some barely passed. I was one of the younger persons in the class. Say no more, that was the truth. I was only nine when I made my Confirmation because I might miss it. My age got changed so that I could make it with Pat. A rule of the religion was that you had to be ten to make your Confirmation, I didn't change my religion for my Confirmation, but my age got changed so that I could make it with Pat.

We went in the pony and trap. Everyone had a red ribbon around their neck with their Confirmation medal and everyone had a ticket on their back. They were postcard size, four by six-inch tickets. On the ticket or card was written your name and address, also your grade, 1st, 2nd or 3rd. And it was signed by the particular person that gave you the examination. And you were graded by a colour. People who got 1st grade in their exam would get a number 1, that was a red ticket, and it had all your particulars written on it. The person who got a 2nd got a blue ticket, it had the same writings and particulars, but it was a second class ticket. The 3rd was yellow, and that was a third class ticket. Everyone passed and received Confirmation and the same sacrament, but people were qualified according to the marks they received in their exam. I got a blue ticket. Around my neck I had the ribbon and the Confirmation medal that was hanging on my chest, and my ticket was on my back for everyone to see. But, not only was my birthday wrong but my ticket was wrong as well. I ended up with Pat Lynam's name on me. There was a bit of a mix up.

There were special people taken in at the end of the ceremony who had applied for Confirmation. They went to a special after-hours class - from a religious point of view - in order to be confirmed. These were people who would have applied for Confirmation; they were adults who had missed out in earlier years.

When the Confirmation ceremony was over we went back home, had dinner and then got on with the jobs.

The smells and tastes of cooking and baking and flying potatoes too

Mother did all the cooking and baking on the open fire. As I explained before, she baked in different sized ovens, cast iron ovens, with legs. When bread was made it was left outside to cool. I remember hearing from Mary that one day they were home, but the door was closed. They could see through the window that my mother had baked and they were starving. Well, they couldn't get into the house and they noticed that the window was a little open. They got an old piece of wire and they got it down onto the table and took the buns out through the window. My mother could never understand where the buns had got to, as nobody had been into the house.

There was another time that my mother and father went into town. My mother had put on the open fire, a big pot of potatoes for us. After the dinner, we were to put on the potatoes for the pigs, a big pot of rubbishy potatoes. Anyway a row started inside over such a one doing such a thing to such a one, and whose turn it was to do this or that. Well, someone got the better of the other with some remark. The big pot of potatoes was in the middle of the floor and I don't know who it was, but up they got and had a go at the other person with a potato. Next thing another potato came flying and the other ducked. Now the walls at home, inside, were always snow-white with whitewash. Next thing a potato was flying and banging off the whitewash, well, around one particular back wall. And what did we do? There was all this shouting "It was all your fault" and "You started it, and "He did this" and "You did that" and it went on like that until we all started crying 'cause Mother and Father would be home from town, any minute. And so everyone got down to clean the floor and clean the walls and we put everything in the rubbishy pot for the pigs. But I'll never forget it; I can still see the potatoes flying in all directions.

In trouble

I can only remember once being slapped by my parents. My mother slapped me on the back of the hand. She got a hold of me by the three fingers and she slapped me on the back of the hand. I was always a tease, but there is one thing that I can still see where I did extremely wrong, and I was chastised for it, and rightly so. Our land ran from high land to low land, and down in the low land there would be rivers, little rivers. We'd call them rivers, but they were really only drains. In the low land in the wintertime, horses would be reaching in from one field to another, to get all the nice soft green grass that would be on top of it. The odd time they would get stuck in the middle of a river or drain.

I went down one evening and I found this mare, a female horse, near the drain. And I went home and I said to Mother "The mare is in the drain down there". She got excited and anxious, she got an awful fright, and my father wasn't around. She said "Run over for your Uncle Pat", Uncle Pat would have lived close by, and someone else and someone else and "Tell them, so that we can get the people together and have people and big ropes to pull the mare out of the drain". Well, I went back before it all started. I said "Sorry Mother its only a big joke", I was trying to tell her I had been exaggerating. Now that's all that happened, and that's all I did. But it was very wrong, very wrong. And I got smacked for it. My father, he called me in the evening and he told me "Never, never, never, do that again", and I don't know whether he gave me a slap on the face or where else, but there was no more to it. And I'm not joking I knew that I got off lightly because I did a terrible thing, I had really given my mother such a terrible fright.

I'd hope and I'd pray that I would give least possible problems to my parents. God knows they had problems enough without my little bits and pieces. I felt and I have pride in that I think that I didn't give them many problems.

The fairies, forts and stories

You could never cross a fairy rath[20] to another fairy rath. We knew where the fairy raths were. We had a fairy fort on the land and of course it was something you wouldn't plough or disturb, for fear of disturbing the fairies. Our fort was on the bend of the road, just after 'the cup and saucer', on the bend of the road going towards Baltrasna. Well, sometimes at night, if we knew there was someone on the road, we'd go out behind the ditch. As they'd turn the bend by the trees, we'd make noises and rattle bottles as we ran over the hill of the fort and down the other side. We'd scare the living daylights out of them.

My father had stories of the fairies. There was one story about a particular night, my father was playing cards in a neighbours house, Byrne's house, the two Byrnes were living in the house at the time, less that a quarter of a mile away, near Baltrasna. They were all playing cards. With that there was a knock or a noise outside, then a bit of a hush. And then the door flew open, and the geese that were in the yard flew into the house, and flew out through a window. There was all a bit of a terrible flutter. After a while the man of the house, the old man of the house said, "Play on the cards now lads, it's all over". So they continued whatever game they were at, and they played on the cards. That's my father's version of what happened in this particular house, and I knew the house very well. They said it was the fairies passing.[21]

---

[20] A fairy rath, also known as a fairy fort, is a circular earthen mound, with reputations of supernatural activity. The Tuatha de Danaan, famous for their skill in magic and other arts, inhabited Ireland before the Celts. There are many legends about the last battles between the two races, with gods and goddesses participating on both sides. Eventually the Celts won, but such was their respect for their opponents that they divided Ireland equally between them, well, nearly equally: the Celts got the upper half and the Tuatha de Danaan got the lower half, so this bright people retreated below ground and became fairies. They are still a formidable race, nearly as big as humans and very proud. The entrances to their main places or 'fairy forts' are in prehistoric burial mounds, which look like little hills with a passage inside, or in circular earthen grass-covered banks, called 'raths'. (These are the remains of what were once protective enclosures for animals and houses.) It is believed that fairies and humans can co-exist peacefully, but fairies have to be treated with great respect. If they get angry they are not slow to take revenge. It was completely taboo to interfere in any way with what were considered to be fairy dwellings. Either you, your family or your cattle would certainly suffer, as thousands of stories show.

[21] Where the Byrnes lived is right beside Jim and Philo's house at Baltrasna. Their house was built between the corner of Byrne's yard and the Blue Stream. Jim never feared the fairies and he is one of the few people who levelled a fairy fort on his land.

But that could be anything I suppose, but those were the sorts of stories that went around. Sure I suppose I told stories myself. You'd be passing by a fairy fort in the country, you might say, in a very deep and serious voice, like you were beginning a very serious story "Well, this was a lonely part of the road... especially at this corner" and you'd add such and such. Sure we'd add to the story for fun, some people wouldn't like that. But that's what the fairies and fairy stories are all about.

Do you know this story of the fairies? I learned it when I was about five or six years of age.

'In his shady nook, one moonlit night,
A leprechaun I did spy.
He'd a scarlet cap, and a coat of green,
And a crúiscín by his side.

As he hammered and sang in his tiny voice,
And he drank his mountain dew,
I laughed to think of the purse of gold,
But the fairy was laughing too.

In quick toe step and in beating heart
Quite softly I drew nigh.
There was a twinkle in his merry face
And a twinkle in his eye.

I asked him for the fairy purse,
"The fairy purse?" he cried.
"The purse" he said, "is in her hand,
The lady by your side."

I turned to look; the elf was gone,
And ah, what was I to do?
I laughed to think of the purse of gold,
But the fairy was laughing too.'

I learned that when I was about five or six years of age.

Summer Holidays

As I said we went every year on our summer holidays to our grandparents in Multifarnham. Josie was living there with my grandparents, Aunt Rose, and my two uncles. I don't know at what age she went down, but she didn't come back to Marlinstown till she was nearly fifteen. It was such a huge treat to go to Ballinreddra on holidays. Pat and I would go. What I remember about the summers was fishing and shooting and making hay, and work and sunshine. We had a great time with Uncle Jack and Uncle Tom, my mother's brothers. My grandmother use to say 'daughteen', she'd say that to all women. Its funny, the one thing I don't understand was that if the uncles did any wrong on us I'd say 'I'm going to tell on you when I go in'. I laugh, imagine threatening their parents on them, on my uncles Uncle Pat and Uncle Tom, that's Pat Loughrey's father.

In Multifarnham we used to have to go to the lake for drinking water, it was about a mile down to Lough Derravaragh. We had no spring water near the house and we used to go to the well down beside the lake for a barrel of water. We used to fill the barrel with spring water and bring it back up on the back of the pony and cart. And we'd go again when the barrel would be finished. The water from the well beside the lake was for drinking, we had rain water for washing, Water would be gathered from the galvanised roofs and the thatched roofs, barrels would be catching the rain off them, all the time.

I didn't think of my grandparents as old. My grandparents were very active and very intelligent. My grandfather was wonderful with his hands, he made all his own farm implements, anything made with wood, no problem. He made gates and doors and all that. He had planes, and screwdrivers and screws and all sorts and types of carpenter's tools, my grandfather had them all then. He had a carpenter's shed out the back and he would be making all those things, we could just see them all there. He made furniture, like what you'd see people putting up on the roadside today, like stools, armchairs. He did all that. I did it myself too at Mullingar Tech. There were no electrical tools; there was no electricity. There were chisels, he'd sharpen his own chisels and they'd be like a lance - for mortising, and all that.

My grandmother was a lovely person, always so kind to you and looking out for you. Well, she didn't work on the farm and you'd never find her doing the milking. She'd take part in the house and take part in the churning[22] time, sure I suppose she was an old woman and was passed her working life. Uncle Jack and Uncle Tom were, I suppose, nearly forty years of age. The churning was always done at lunchtime, when the men would be in for their

---

[22] Churning of butter.

lunch. They had a dash churn.[23] You'd have the milk all ready and separated and when the men would be finished their lunch, they would each take their turn at the dash.[24] At home in Marlinstown we had an end over end churn, we were very mod. They were made by Pierces of Wexford. You could see them hanging over a hedge today sometimes if your passing through the country, or maybe in an antique shop.

My grandparents didn't sing or tell stories; they used to listen to the crickets. Did you ever see crickets?

In the evening time we'd be hoping that after they'd be saving the corn or sacking the oats, and if it was a nice fine evening and early enough, that we could get around Uncle Tom or Uncle Jack or maybe the both of them to go down to the lake to go fishing. We would be getting all hot and bothered about going fishing. It was a bit of a distance down from the house to Derravaragh Lake and we would go fishing there with worms and we'd fish and catch perch.

We would often go out fishing on the boat. The midges would always be out. I remember that Uncle Tom and Jack they'd be fishing at the top of the boat and we would be at the side of the boat with weights – stones or a bit of lead at the end of a hand line. The first thing you'd have to do was to find the depth of the water, and then you would want to let your line go down a foot or two less. You'd be there for a while leaning over the side of the boat. The next thing you'd feel a bit of a nibble on your line, and next a bit of a pull on it, and you'd pull up the fish and then put it into the old bucket that would be there on the boat. I remember one evening catching twenty-one perch. As fast as you were pulling them in, you were taking them out; they'd bite anything. They were very scaly; they had a lot of scales on them. But you'd eat them alright. Perch is a beautiful sweet fish. There were perch and roach, but it was perch that we always caught.

The uncles fished with a rod, a hazel rod. Hazel would be growing on the side of the shore. At a place called the Culliens there was a great plantation of nuts, a plantation of hazel, of thick hazel rod. You'd get plenty of straight ones, as straight as the ash I have growing at the front of the house in Palmerstown, except they were hazel. The uncles would have a line, a fishing line with maybe a bit of gut at the top with hooks. They would put worms on the hooks. They'd cast out and be watching the cork going away and then they'd pull it in

---

[23] A dash churn was a tall, narrow, nearly cylindrical wooden tub, fitted with a wooden cover. The cream in the churn was agitated by a hand operated vertical plunger or dash.

[24] It is harder work than the end-over-end churn. The dash has to be vigorously thumped up and down by hand, to make the cream coagulate into butter.

regularly. They'd feed a worm onto the hook every time they'd take the line out of the water. We would have a can of worms, crawling alive from the garden. We'd dig them up and put them in the can with a bit of clay. We'd nearly always go home with a bucket of fish.

Sunday was always a day of rest. At that time you were only allowed work on a Sunday if the weather was bad, if there had been a bad spell of weather. We would go off on Sunday after mass, shooting rabbits - about two hours after mass. On a Sunday too, we would go pike fishing in the middle of the lake. My uncles would row the boat up and down the lake, we would have spinners, probably one line on each side of the boat and we'd use the spinners. We would often catch three pike. We would eat them for tea in the evening. The women would wash them and clean them and look after them.

Halloween

At Halloween we played games. Apples on a string and money in a bucket were the favourites. You would put a string through the centre of an apple and tie a big knot at the end. You'd tie the string to the ceiling. You'd have to bite into the apple with you arms behind your back. It was difficult enough to get a bite, especially the first bite, when you would have to bite into the skin. The apple would be swinging from side to side, or around your face. With money in a bucket, well, we put the money in a basin quarter full of water, and you'd have to put your face right in to try to pick up the money with your mouth.

Snow and frosty mornings

There were drains on the land between fields, like little rivers, we called them drains. They were about two or three feet wide. We would play games jumping drains at a point, sometimes they were narrower at a point and it was easy to cross. Sometimes you'd be too small to cross and the other lads would be gone ahead and they would have to come back for you, to get you across at a spot that would be narrow.

Sometimes, after a lot of rain, drains would spill over and go out over the land in a little channel, there might be a little gap and the water would flow out on the shallow part of the field alongside it. In the winter we'd be looking forward to the frost catching up on the drains and freezing up. We would make a nice skid along that, like in a little dip in the ground. You would go in your strong boots and slide on the ice.

Snowball games we played on the way to school. You'd be on one side of the road and others on the other side, you'd duck and the next minute you'd get a snowball in the forehead. The girls didn't play; well, they did, if there was any one of them tough enough to keep up with the lads, and to put up with it. Girls were, and are as good as the lads, if they get wound up to it. None of ours were interested anyway, not Josie, or Teresa, well, she was very small anyway, and Mary wasn't interested. They weren't into games or anything like that. There were a few tough ones though, of course there were, I don't remember their names.

We used to pass Glennon's house going to school. It was the place to go if there had been a fierce frost the night before. If there was a hard frost, or if it was freezing, you'd head for Glennon's for a slide. At lunchtime you'd have a half-hour for lunch. You'd dash down out of school and away for about half a mile, down the road into Glennon's field, into Glennon's yard, and then out the back where there was another gate and then you'd get into the haggard. Out beyond there was another house, and there behind it, was a little valley of water, that had come off a river. The car road went around it. We would go around the car-road to get to the water.

It took us ten minutes to run down from school, and ten minutes to run back. If we could get ten minutes on the slide it was great. We would take turns. The slide would be about, well, maybe thirty yards if you were lucky, maybe about twenty yards. You'd be preparing for it, getting a good run at it, so you'd probably only have about twenty yards of a slide and you'd go pel mel.[25] The slide would be only about two feet wide and we'd have it well polished, going on it. We would be one after the other in a line, as soon as one fellow was off, you were off. And we'd be hunker sliding there, really enjoying ourselves. When you'd get to the other side, you'd stand up again and fall out on the grass, and come around to get your chance to go again. It was fantastic to do that for ten or fifteen minutes, to go hunker sliding on the ice.

There is one occasion that I remember well. We were after having a great evening sliding on ice. We decided that we would go to school very early the following morning and get a slide before we started school. Well, Pat was into sliding in a big way. Anyway we got to Glennon's about twenty to ten; we had to be in school at ten o'clock. We went down the lane round the back, through the gate behind the haggard into the little field with the pond where the slide was. I was first out to the slide from the night before. There was nothing on top of it except this trawneen trissy.[26] You know that white frost, you'd often see it, you could rub it off. Well, that type of white frost was on the slide, but still the slide was visible.

---

[25] Go really fast.

[26] Traneen trissy is white frost, like a soft moss. You often see it on the branch of a tree on the morning after a mild to heavy frost. It is so soft though; you'd only have to tap the branch to shake it off.

Well, I went at it and had a good chase at it. I went out sliding on it, flying across it, and came to about four or five foot from the far side, when the ice broke. I was down to my knees and to my top-stockings in icy water. And every time I put up my foot, it went down again through the ice. The ice was broken and I had to walk the last five-foot in the water, well, ice and water, it was frozen. And then I had to make my way up to school, wearing strong boots and they full of water, and the perishing was atrocious. So then when we were taking out schoolbooks what we were looking for was paper. I took off the boots and poured out the water and then took off my stockings and rang them out. Well, I wrapped my legs, bandaged my legs in papers, in school copy pages or anything that you could tear leaves out of, so that I could put that around my legs and pull up my stockings up over them. Then they would be at least half-dry, before you would go home in the evening.

There was no real heat in the school, there might be a bit of heat up around the turf fire, but the school room, the one room in the school, was about forty feet long. Every other class, a stand-up class would get a chance to stand around the fire, but there was no such thing as heat, not at all. There was a turf shed outside the schoolroom. We didn't each bring a sod of turf a day. Someone would bring a load of turf for a day or a week; some would be good turf, some dry turf. Some people might be closer to the bog than others and they might have more turf than we had or others had, and they would bring turf to the school. But there was no such thing as heat as we know it.

Christmas A time of complete fill up of excitement

Christmas was a time when you worked like hell to have everything done before Christmas. And we had our own jobs to do, at five and six and seven, and quite a lot of them, with cows and feeding calves. It was a time of complete fill up of excitement. We didn't eat turkeys in those days. We had goose.

The day before Christmas, Christmas Eve, everyone went into town, the whole family, on the pony and trap. You were on the loose as it were, that day. That was the day you could ramble around the town, on Christmas Eve. You had so much money saved up for Christmas and you'd get so much money to spend, and you were really looking forward to this. And you'd be going around buying things, like I'd be buying a mouth organ, or something like that, and you'd be buying things just to make Christmas different.

The first thing we did when we got to town was go to confession, everyone went to confession in preparation for Christmas.

On Christmas Eve night we had a big supper called 'big supper night' and we went into the parlour. And in the big press box in the parlour there would be all the cakes. There would be six or eight saucepan cakes; each child would have its own cake, beautiful saucepan cakes, a rich cake. They were made of plain flour and there would be currants and raisins and maybe, candied peel chopped up in them. They were a pound weight or there abouts. There would be a lovely pale crust on them when they would be taken out of the oven.

They would be left out for us. And we would have this tea, and you'd get your saucepan cake, and you'd cut it, and your cake might last you two or three days. Mother used to make the saucepan cakes. The saucepans were made of tin, and they were made by the tinkers, they made the saucepans. They would hold a pint, and they had handles on them. The saucepan cakes were baked in an ordinary cast-iron pot oven, with four legs under it, and with 'grisha'.

At Christmas we drank lemonade. We called it 'spurt'. We had a couple of soda streams at Christmas with lemonade in them and that was our treat for Christmas. My father didn't drink, I suppose only once in a blue moon. He might go to a coursing match and he might come home with a few drinks in him. On my mother's side they didn't drink much either, my Uncle Tom or Jack wouldn't have taken drink as such, maybe a glass of wine and my grandfather didn't drink.

At Christmas time the house wouldn't be decorated, there was nothing like that, but there would be holly, plenty of holly.

Christmas morning we generally went to first mass, nine o'clock. When we got home after mass we'd have our breakfast in the parlour and the table would be all set up in the parlour. And what did we have for breakfast? Mutton chops. I can always remember them as being fat, never very lean, they were like loin chops, mutton chops, and that was Christmas morning. After that we'd get out and we'd tidy up around the yard and whatever had to be done and we'd go off then hunting foxes.

Hunting Foxes

We'd hear about foxes over in the bank or over in the ditch 'cause feathers would have been seen scattered around. We'd go off and try to dig them out. If it was a soft ditch we might be lucky. Sometimes the ditch would be full of tree roots and briars and hard earth and it would be too difficult to dig. We'd have someone there with a gun to shoot them and kill them. Some fella might have a ferret, but that would be a rarity. First you'd dig out the bank. Then you'd get a big, big long thorny briar and you'd stick that up into the middle of the burrow, to find the direction of the burrow. Foxes might go in at one angle and then they could go off in another direction, it could be misleading. You'd have a crowbar and you'd bore a hole with the crowbar, down into the ground. You'd stick the briar down this hole. If it would come up with any hairs on it you'd know you were near enough to where the foxes were, or you would know at least that there could be foxes in there. When you'd worked out where you thought the fox was, you'd dig out a hole behind the fox, you'd collapse the tunnel and you'd block off all his other possible exits. This way you'd hunt him out. The fox would finally have to come out where it went in.

The fox would come out and go mad across the country and the dogs would follow and there would be a hunt and that would be it. But I can't ever remember catching foxes. It was a bit of sport, there were times that you'd spend the whole day trying to dig out a fox and you'd never even find him. But I do know that if you chased them out of the area they were gone. You'd know you'd had foxes 'cause you'd be after missing three geese, or hens or chickens. Sometimes you'd go hunting foxes on a Sunday. You might see a couple of lads going off and you'd ask if you could come along and you'd bring a couple of spades or a shovel or a crowbar with you. Poor old fox. My father never came with us, he might be at home reading a book, or 'Our Boys' or 'Red Letter' or something like 'Irelands Own'.

Easter Sunday was a great day for eating eggs. I remember one Easter, Pat ate thirteen eggs. There was always loads of eggs, and you'd see who could eat the most. You had to eat the egg from Good Friday first, that one would have been marked with soot. That one was fried on the pan. About fifty eggs at a time were cooked in a skillet pan on Easter Sunday and you'd cut them down the middle, I remember on this particular Easter Sunday, I sat on one side of the table and Pat on the other, I stopped after eating eleven eggs and Pat went on to eat thirteen. After eating the eggs, you'd go outside and go into the hayshed and you'd go up the ladder. Half way up, at about eight feet high you'd go into a big bench of hay and fall asleep.

We had two greyhounds at home. About a mile across the fields from our place was Leavey's. He was a farmer who had an abattoir; he had a butcher's shop in Mullingar. Well, I would get four cow shins from him and we'd boil them up for the greyhounds, they would make a really thick jelly, and we would feed that to the greyhounds with brown bread. Beyond in Leavey's field was where some great matches were played. There was one field with short grass in it, a square field. It would be all marked out the morning of a match and there would be people doing stewarding. It was great craic. The Mental Hospital might be playing the Downes. We would be young and doing loads of running around and we would head over to see those matches. There was no hurling around the Downes.

WHEN MY FATHER DIED

I remember when my father died.[27] He died in hospital. I was twelve years old. The funeral went to Mullingar; the funeral mass was in the church in the town. The cathedral wouldn't have been finished then. I can barely remember the funeral; we just went in a car. At the time, the funeral mass would have been in the morning and the burial in the afternoon. It was the custom then that women did not attend the burial. My mother would not have gone to my father's burial in Killucan.

My father died of ... You ask what he died of? Hard work I suppose, but really I don't know what it was, I remember him having a bad flu. That's about as much as I could say now on that. He had been sick for a while. If that was today he would not have died.

But we had such fantastic times, great memories. When I think of all the things that were done on the farm when my father was alive, and we must have been really tiny. I have such wonderful memories. And we would be working out on the farm all day on a Saturday, weeding turnips and all sorts of things, at nine, ten years of age. You'd work all day with the men; you'd do the lighter work at the end of the row.

There wasn't loads of contact with my father's side, but my father's brothers and sisters would come back to do the rounds, where they grew up as children. My mother's closest friend, who was always there for her, was Aunt Agnes in Mullingar. She was married to my father's brother, Uncle Mike. My mother was also very close and very fond of her sister Rose; she was only thirty-three or thirty five when she died of cancer. Aunt Rose loved 'Skipper sardines' the ones with the picture of the man with the hat. My mother would always send you for a tin of sardines when Aunt Rose was coming to visit.

We were naturally connected to Multifarnham; we had a personal connection to Multifarnham. Josie, as I said, went to live with our grandparents, Aunt Rose and our uncles when she was quite young. She came back to Marlinstown when she was fifteen. Rose then went to Ballinreddra. She was five years old when she was sent down, she didn't come back home until she was fourteen. She went to school in Multifarnham; she was never at school in Curraghmore. She did the baking and the cooking. Aunt Rose, mother's sister, died when Rose was nine. Rose could tell you stories, and about making flap-jacks with rhubarb or apples and bringing the tea to the men working in the fields or saving hay. She would make the tea, put it into a bucket, put straw all around the bucket to keep the bucket warm and then put the warm flap-jacks on a plate, on top of the bucket,

---

[27] Bill Lynam died on 21 March 1931, aged 57. He was born on 25 June 1873.

and then carry the whole lot out to feed the men and she'd have a pile of mugs as well. The one job that Rose said she really hated doing was washing eggs.

When we were growing up we had connections to my father's family we'd spend our holidays between my father's side and my mother's side. Aunt Mary Cunningham, my father's sister always came to Marlinstown on holidays and stayed three or four days. She was the first person I ever saw take an injection.[28] We'd stand around her with her little files, she'd say "Say a prayer for Aunt Cunney."

I was saying I don't remember much of my father's funeral, but I do know that afterwards, work just had to go on. We weren't in the dairy business then, at the time that my father died.

After my father died it was difficult for my mother. It was tough, really tough. But if you'd ever need advice there were always neighbours there, and you would always have some friend who would come along and help you out. Uncle Pat and Aunt Bridie were there if you needed them. "If you ever have a problem Mrs Lynam we are there to help you out" - that's the word that would have gone around. People were and are very kind. It was difficult for my mother, as a woman, it sure was. It sure, sure was. Women were treated as they are normally treated. It's just too bad that they don't get the respect that they deserve. All women, I say that all the time, all the time.

We wouldn't have known anything about what was going on. At that time children were never allowed to listen to adults' conversation when adults were talking, you were always sent outside. If anyone came to the house, if some man, woman or child came into the house you would be sent off out. They might be talking about someone down the road, about someone who had died, about someone who had got married, or about land, but you never heard or were told anything about it. You certainly weren't allowed listen. You never heard about adults' disappointments, or worries, or disagreements. Parents never talked in front of their children about their problems. God knows my mother would have had big worries after my father died, but you would never hear anything about it.

Mary was five and Teresa was three when my father died. They went to stay with Aunt Lizzie and Uncle John McCormack out on the main road. Rose was down in Ballinreddra. Uncle John McCormack used to drive young horses, and a bad car, and he'd be out in the middle of the road going pel mel and a mile a minute. Mary remembers a day when a horse ran away, with she and young Teresa and Aunt Lizzie in the trap. Uncle John had said

---

[28] Aunt Cunney was a diabetic.

"Hell, heaven or Dundalk" and he'd let the horse away. And as they went down the Dublin bridge, Mary remembers Aunt Lizzie trying to jump off, the horse was gone pure mad. Paddy Crowley took off his coat and pegged it on the horse's head. They were fond of Uncle John, he was kind. He had a good farm of land and was very fond of horses. He knew a lot about them and he himself had a lot of control over horses, he wasn't afraid of horses. He'd put a horse under a mowing machine and get away with it.

Living with Aunt Lizzie was different for Mary and Teresa, and they too had their work cut out for them and their jobs on Saturdays. Mary talks of Aunt Lizzie's plates, she had her wall decorated with fine big dishes, big vegetable dishes and Mary would have to go out and get the finest grains of sand outside amongst the gravel outside the house and shine all the plates. She claims to clearly see the sand still. Aunt Lizzie entertained a lot at home. She often sent out gold edged invitations. Some people thought she had great notions about herself. But she was very different in manner to Uncle John, she was so refined and spoke with an accent. He was a big rough-cut man and could let out the odd swear. In Aunt Lizzie's house, children were not given tea; you might only get an egg-cup-full, that used to kill Mary.

Josie went to England. Well, the way it happened was, the Cunninghams felt that the Lynams coming up needed to be helped to get fixed up in a job or a trade. They were inclined in helping that way and Josie was always interested in baking and all that sort of thing. She was sent over to her first cousin Kate Folston in Hull. Josie was only fifteen or sixteen years of age and she went over there to serve her time to the confectionery trade. I remember she worked in the bake house. She was great for the first few years. The Folstons were big in confectionery, it wasn't a shop and they had a few staff working for them.

One day, Mother got a letter to say Josie was coming home and that her health wasn't the best. I didn't know the whole story but I remember my mother with tears leaving her eyes. "Mother don't let it worry you and Please God everything's going to be alright". My mother threw her arms around me and said "Tom you're most consoling and you're always there to help me" or something like that. I can still see this all happening. Josie came home anyway, she wasn't well and she had to get so much rest and mother took it to heart.

Going to school in the sand-hole of knowledge

Curraghmore was known by everybody that went to the school as 'the sand-hole of knowledge'. It was in the area of a sandpit. Curraghmore was a big school with a big room. As I was telling you before, it was about thirty five or forty feet long. There was no partition in the middle of the room, there was no division in the centre, there weren't two rooms. I think there were forty-five or fifty pupils, boys and girls.

It was never noisy, at school you would be only talking to be heard. When you were around the map it would be the same. While we were at the map, other people would be doing their writing. Normally you finished at fourteen years of age.

The head teacher, the head mistress was in the top class and she would be looking after fourth to sixth classes. The junior teacher would be looking after junior infants up to fourth class. You were divided into age groups to a certain point. We all got taught the same thing; some people were helped along. But if you weren't able to move from third class to fourth class, if you weren't able for fourth class, you would be left another year in third class. The inspector would come around and pass you into fourth class from third class. From fourth class you went up a class every year. If you didn't make the grade to get by, you were left in that class for another year, and then you could move on. And you qualified as you went up. Some people got out of school early 'cause they were brighter than others.

The whole thing was to get out of school, and get finished with school by the time you were fourteen years of age, or fifteen. There was never really any talk of going on at school. It was a question of really getting it finished. Parents might take you out of school, but in my time no one was ever taken out of school and sent on to college or anything like that. The only time anyone left our school was to be kept at home to do work.

If it was a good national school, that's where you were sent and you were left on there, and it was considered as good as the rest. And if there was a good teacher there, that was it. Our teachers were considered good. The teacher's children went to the school, her children went on, one of them became a chemist.

You had your home exercise to do, headlines and writing was very much part of your education. You had to do writing and it had to be up to a standard in class and you'd certainly get biffed if your writing wasn't good. Some fellas' copies you'd think the hens got onto them, with all the marks on their copies, you'd wonder who, or what, had walked across them.

I liked arithmetic best. I was fairly good at arithmetic. But you never really got a chance. You talk about algebra, well, we only just got a glimpse of algebra and that was only in sixth standard. We had a half-hour of history, up in front of the map. And a half-hour of this or that. It was all very simple. Our teachers would not have matched Mr Noone,[29] or other teachers I would have heard about, there was no talk of poetry, or anything like that.

If we had been in school in Mullingar we would have been treated differently. Where we were, it was a country school, they were dealing with farmers and the attitude was, you were farmers' children.

I suppose the point was, you were going to the local school and you would get all the knowledge you could for the first five or six years 'cause you were to be reared up in the country life. And when you came to the age of fourteen you'd be out 'cause there was loads of work to be done at home. But you probably could have been taken out from an ordinary national school and sent on into the Christian Brothers, it would depend really on making provisions for your livelihood, by having yourself better educated.

At fourteen, if you were a farmer's son, you were like an absolute tradesman to a farmer, and very valuable, you would have been well trained in from a very early age into farming and all to do with it. And so you left school at fourteen. Then, when you came to the age of sixteen or eighteen years of age, at that time, and at that age, you branched out to do something different in the farming line or went on to do a very ordinary job because you hadn't got the schooling, or the ability, or you hadn't the qualifications, or the contacts, or you couldn't think or hope to be able to do anything else. Farmers' daughters went to Dublin to serve their time in the drapery business. You had to put down a fee, pay a fee to the company to take you on as an apprentice. No matter what you wanted to do, you had to serve your time to it, in the grocery trade, as a blacksmith, whatever.

I ended up being fourteen, when I was really only thirteen, and leaving school when I was really only thirteen years of age. This happened because they had changed my birthday that time, so that I would make my Confirmation with Pat. Oh I would have loved the opportunity to stay on in school. I stayed at home from school early to help at home and that's for sure. And it was appreciated. But I would have much preferred, and it was an easier job, to go to school than to stay at home and work on the farm.

---

[29] Mr Noone was the headmaster in the national school in Boston, Co Clare where Treasa and her sisters and brother went to school. He was of the old school, he promoted the Irish language, a classical education, a dislike of the historical British yoke, poetry that glorified the Gael, history and geography of the world and the myths and legends of the classical warriors of Greece and Rome. Considered a fine teacher by many, some of his 'teaching' methods would be unacceptable today.

Setting up the Dairy

In my case when I left school at thirteen years of age, it was a very, very rough, perishable, cold and miserable life for everyone concerned, and for the farmer. We went through the economic war and the land annuities.[30] People ask, "How do you know so much about politics?" Well, you knew more about politics than you did about school. Everywhere you were going, there were people fighting for a shilling.

I was twelve when my father died, when I think of my poor mother and all she had to contend with, there were eight children, five of them under ten, and Teresa the youngest was only three years of age. When Pat took over the farm he was fourteen. He wasn't able to saddle a horse. He had to get a box to raise him up.

I remember when I left school, someone had the wild idea of delivering and selling milk. I went into Mullingar and canvassed around Mullingar to see who would take milk from me if I delivered it on a given day. I got someone to buy for me up in Dublin, a pint tin and a half-pint tin and the can with a spout on it. And then I had to have a churn to hold a quantity of milk. I got a tap put on the side of the churn, that I could just turn on or off.

When I started I would go in with the pony and trap or a spring car.[31] I'd have buttermilk as well. Then I got to the stage where I might sell four or five gallons of milk, you were put to it 'cause neighbour told neighbour and I ended selling up to fifteen or twenty gallons of milk. I only had three or four cows and if a cow went off milk, when she would go dry, I'd have to have another cow to take her place. And then if a cow was calving I might have to buy milk off somebody else to keep up the supply. I'd sell it for tuppence halfpenny. There was little or no profit in it; it was just a way of changing a pound. Cows at that time were four and five and six pounds each, I remember the best of cattle, the best of cattle sold for seven pounds, ten shillings. The same cattle today would be seven hundred pounds.

---

[30] Land annuities were the money that the British government had loaned to Irish farmers before the Government of Ireland Act 1921 and which the farmers had agreed to pay back. Part of the Anglo-Irish Treaty was that the Free State would collect the debts and return the money to Britain. When De Valera came to power for the first time in 1932 he refused to hand over the money. The British imposed a 20% tariff on trade with the Free State. Ireland could no longer sell its beef in the Six Counties (Northern Ireland) or in Britain. Ireland retaliated by imposing a tariff in the opposite direction. There was an expression at the time - 'Burn everything British except its coal'. The economic war lasted till 1938 when De Valera paid over 10 million pounds to Britain and in return Britain pulled out of her naval bases in Ireland.

[31] A spring cart.

Old Mrs Moore, she'd bring in buttermilk, she parked down in Mount Street and people would come to her there. Kit Dalton of Curraghmore then started the milk, it was at the same time, and she'd go to Patrick Street.

At the time of the year when we had a garden of cabbage I'd go into town on a Saturday with the cart full of cabbage and try and sell them at two pence a head.

Once I remember coming out home from town, after delivering the milk, I was in the trap with the pony. I'd a lovely chestnut pony, a great stepper. I was coming down Mary Street, passing Byrne's, and I decided we're on our way home now. I was finished and I was getting good movement coming around to the calf market there. I just got down about ten or twelve yards down Mary Street and I saw two policemen coming past Mullalley's. They stepped out from Gibney's corner, I'm nearly sure that's what it was then, and they crossed out in front of me. As a result I had to pull the reigns to hold back the pony. I was going fairly fast. Well, as I did pull the reigns, the pony lost her footing. She fell forward, broke the two shafts of the car, and got trapped in the harness and cut her shin. I was left in the car with the two policemen looking back at me. That happened coming home after delivering all the milk. I probably brought the trap down to Fairley's in Blackhall, he'd have put the car together, fixed it for me and made me new shafts. The wheels and everything else were all right. I think that experience was in the daylight, and in the summer time of the year. I must have got an awful shock. What happened the pony that night, and how I got home the same night, I can't really remember. But I remember the policemen didn't even come back to lift me up, or to see if I was OK. But what a mess, what a mess.

There is one morning I particularly remember. It was after the night of the big snow. It was in 1932, I'm nearly sure it was that year 'cause my father didn't live to see that big snow. We had a fall of snow that would have been about four feet high, and where the snow would have blown into a corner, the snow would have been up to ten feet high. The canal was iced over. Coming back from Mullingar that morning after delivering the milk, it was blowing a terrible blizzard, it was something desperate. You could take the snow out of the sockets in your eyes like snowballs. The two cans on the cart were full of ice. The cart was in a cover of ice. I thought if we stopped we'd die and perish. The chestnut pony saved my life. The pony kept going. I came back into the yard but I couldn't get down through the yard to the house. I had to first look after the pony that I was driving. I have memories of climbing over big high mounds of snow in the yard. Later we dug trenches and we thought it was great gas altogether, digging trenches down to the ground through the snow. It was great fun for the smaller ones running through the snow trenches like a maze.

They were very tough times. Aunt Rose, Mother's sister died in 1933, two years after my father died, and she left £300 (three hundred pounds) to my mother. For some reason or other, my mother never got the money then. Jim used to say that with it she would have been able to get more than thirty cows and have set up and properly established the dairy. £10 (ten pounds) would have bought the finest cow in 1933. If she had got the money at that time Jim felt that the family would have been all right and everyone would have been set up. [32]

We had to leave, and head off to make a life. There was only room for one at home and the rest would all move on. I did the milk and then went to Dublin. Then Bill did the milk after me and then followed me to Dublin. He followed a few years after. I know he would have liked to have stayed in Marlinstown. He went off working for a farmer milking cows only a few miles out of Dublin, a big dairy farmer who supplied milk to the city of Dublin. Later he worked as a gardener in Stillorgan. Later again he got into working with wood; he was gifted at that.

I remember going back to Mullingar years later. I used to be asked if I was the Buttermilk Lynam. I'd trace it and realise it was Bill they were talking about. I started delivering the milk and was doing it for three years before going to Dublin. I knew Mullingar like the back of my hand from doing the milk, nobody knew me, but everyone knew Bill - the milkman. I always felt that I was too young when I was sent away. I missed out on so much in Mullingar.

I went to Mullingar Tech for a while. A year or two after I left school I went to a woodwork class. The class was at seven o'clock in evening in the Technical School in the town. I would go in on the pony and trap. I remember I made a dresser in the woodwork class, drawers and all. I brought it home and it was put in the kitchen and replaced the old dresser. Bill went to the night classes too. When Josie came back from Hull and got better, she went to the Tech for a short while before she went off to Dublin. Rose too went to the Tech for nearly a year when she came back from Ballinreddra. When she was fifteen she went to Dublin. I was already about four years in Dublin at that stage.

---

[32] On the day of this conversation between Tom and Philo, 1 May 2003, they also discussed the current price and value of cattle. The day before, Noel, Jim and Philo's son, had gone into Swarbrigg's in Mullingar to buy a pair of children's runners. A pair of runners cost Euro 140. "God" says Noel "the price of a calf, that's all a calf is worth these days, the same as the price of a pair of child's runners".

Pat and Tom and the 'old cart'.

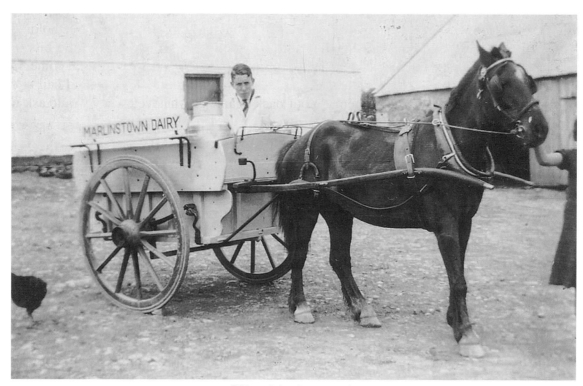

Bill and the 'new cart'.

The Tinkers

A tinker family would camp out our road; it was only a narrow country road. They weren't called Travellers then. You didn't ever call them gypsies, they were always known as tinkers. They would be living in tents, a long tent. If you were coming back after being in Mullingar for the morning, you would turn Nancy's corner and you might see them on the side of the road. You would say "Oh the tinkers are here". You would see the children first. They would be camped at just one particular spot on the road, at Nancy's Corner. And the father of the group would be beside the tent, an open tent. The tent was completely open at one end and you would see the children inside in it. And the mother, she might be holding a baby in her arms, and the other smaller children would be there with the little bits of clothes on them. That would be the morning time and by evening time they would come up around. It would be only every half-mile that they'd meet a house. They would call and you would have a little chat with them, "Your back again" or whatever. They would ask if you wanted any saucepans.

The women did all the selling. The women would have hanks of those saucepans on a piece of material all hanging on their arms, and there would be all sorts of mugs. They would ask for so much and you would pay them what they wanted for them. There was no bargaining but they might throw in a little 'pinny', what was called a 'panny', a little small mug like the size of the ones we have at home today, that was a small saucepan. They also made a big saucepan, like a very large mug that you would have today. But the most popular size was the one that was the same size as today's delph mug. You would drink out of them, but you would also eat out of them. You wouldn't eat your porridge off a plate or a saucer; you'd always eat your porridge out of one of those large saucepans.

When the tinkers would come, you might be looking for something in particular. You would have been waiting for them to come, and you would be waiting for them to come to get something made. You would ask the woman for whatever special thing you wanted her husband to make for you. "I'll bring it to you tomorrow", she might say.

They got on with everyone, and people would never be cross to them. They weren't that type of people. They generally knew where they would be going. When they would leave that spot on the side of the road, where they were after being, you would miss them. The amount of waste that they would have after making all those saucepans would be minimal, you couldn't credit it. There would be no waste. If they had a strip of tin, they would bend it in two, or clip the corners off it and make up a handle out of it. Little strips they would use up, like laces. They were brilliant tradesmen. The wire they would have on the top of a saucepan, was rusty round wire that they would find in a hedge and they would wrap tin around it and cover it. They would blend it in. You could ask them to make anything, big or small and they could make it.

Politics in the family

My mother was reared in the part of the country where I suppose there were strong connections to the basis of Fianna Fáil.[33] There are names that I could tell you about, but you wouldn't really know anything about them, they go back so far.

We would be going as a smaller farmer, but before that we would have voted... well, my mother with Fianna Fáil. But my father would have voted Cumann na nGaedheal.[34] He came from that tradition; it came up with him.

You'd have fellows at election time, and you'd hear "Ah you needn't ask them over there, we know their votes". "Ah Bill Lynam, he's all right for us"
And my mother would shake one of the men's hand and say, "I'll see ye's all right".
"Will we send the car for you anyway" and they would get a drive in the motorcar, about four miles to the polling station in the Downes schoolhouse.

When the Fianna Fáil crowd would come around my mother used to say "Well, Cumann na nGaedheal are paying for my car, but sure you know me". They'd say "Mrs Lynam, we know you, and we know where we stand where you are concerned" And that was all there was about it.

My personal view, I mean my personal view was that the small people, the small farmers and the people working on farms voted for Fianna Fáil. All those people had a vote like anyone else. But you'd find a farmer, a big farmer with about two hundred acres and with six labourers. The man of the house, paying the wages, he'd be Cumann na nGaedheal. The workers that would be working the farm, well, most of them, the small people, the labourers, would be voting Fianna Fáil. Labour was the other party, they had a following, but they were caught between Fianna Fáil and Cumann na nGaedheal and they got little representation. Workers, labourers, most voted Fianna Fáil, not Labour or the Farmers Party and certainly not Cumann na nGaedheal or Fine Gael[35] as they became. It's carried on today.

---

[33] The Republican Party founded by De Valera and others in 1924. The Treaty with Britain, signed in 1922, created a Free State of 26 counties. The partitioning of the country into six and twenty-six counties led to a Civil War between pro and anti Treaty forces.
[34] The pro Treaty party founded in 1923 and led by William T. Cosgrave.
[35] In 1933 Fine Gael, led by General Eoin O'Duffy, was formed from a merger of Cumann na nGaedheal, the

I followed my mother's politics, well, I had a feeling about it, I always had a feeling to be Irish, and a deep love of things Irish and Irish traditions.

The Mental Hospital was out the town

I remember them often bringing coal out to the Mental Hospital. They would be drawing the coal from the railway and there would always be two horses. There was a horse to bring the load of coal up the town, and then a change of horse to bring the load of coal up the Windmill Hill, in order to get it over the hill up to the Hospital. In my father's time the doctors would be responsible in the County Hospital, they were the bosses in the County Hospital… and they were. Many of the people in the hospital were put in as patients because they were a bit of trouble or they gave a bit of trouble, they were thrown aside and put into the Mental Hospital. It could happen to anyone. They got fed over there and that was it. It was a way of getting rid of people as it were. And some of those people were the finest men that ever farmed, a finer class to come off the land you wouldn't find, they were the finest of men. And it was felt why not give these men a little extra status, train them, make them work on the farm. So that's what happened. They put the men out on the farm. A tenant would use the machinery, but the men from the Mental Hospital would tie the oats, and they would do the work on the farm that ordinary farmers' sons would do.

Making and recording the offerings at funerals

Offerings were a big thing in Mullingar, even up to not long ago. I would often be sent to represent the family at funerals. My first memory of the offerings was at a funeral near us. A woman died in the house on her own. The priest rode out on the horse from Mullingar, that was how they travelled in those days. He said the prayers over the corpse of the woman. Outside the cottage was put the table for the offerings with the white cloth on it. It would be a little fold up table like a card table. Someone would provide it, or the person looking after the funeral would bring it. Anyone passing by, put their offering on the table, that meant that you were at the funeral and it was recorded. It went from a shilling up to a pound; a pound would be left by the chief mourners. Well, the priest would take that up and there might be little or nothing in it, but he'd take what was on the cloth and put it in his pocket and ride away. You could blame the priest but that was the custom at the time. In Mullingar they would read out, off the altar, the amount that everyone gave. Well, over a certain amount that was. They didn't read out the poorest offerings.

National Centre Party and the National Guard (The Blueshirts). This followed the banning of a Blueshirts march in August 1933 by De Valera. Fianna Fáil had come to power for the first time in 1932, made possible with support from the Labour Party. In February 1933, de Valera had dismissed Eoin O'Duffy, who was leader of the Blueshirts, from his post as Commissioner of the Gárda Siochána.

The offerings were usually collected at the burial, which would take place in the afternoon. The requiem mass, the mass for the deceased person, would be held in the morning time and everyone could attend that. The men would attend the burial, the odd time a woman would represent her family and bring the offering, if she was a widow woman. I'd have the job of going to bring our family's offering to the funeral. I could also be taking offerings for all the other farmers who couldn't go. I remember once going down to Corralstown to a funeral. I had a bicycle; well, the bicycle would go as long as you kept it going. Do you know when a bike starts missing? When it starts banking, and you can't get it to go without giving it a small bit of a bang with a hammer or a stone? Well, I remember going to that Corralstown funeral with a stone in my pocket. The thing was - as long as I could keep pedalling, I could keep going, but if I stopped I'd have to pull over and give it a bang with a stone. That's why I had the stone in my pocket. I suppose we never had a good bike. I remember going over to Dunne's one night to put two bikes into one. Pat Dunne helped me to do that.

But the offerings! It stopped in Navan many, many moons age ago. How it stopped in Navan was that this man came back after being years, nearly all his life, in America. When he came home they were laying offerings at his mother's funeral and he said, in front of everyone, to the parish priest "Whatever it is you're expecting today at the offerings I'll write you a cheque for it, I'll pay you, you won't auction my mother". That's the way he put it. They say that's when the custom of giving offerings stopped in Navan. There might be offerings three or four miles outside of it, but there were no more offerings in the village of Navan.

It was the way priests got money to live on.

COMING TO DUBLIN

On April Fool's Day I came up to Dublin. The year was 1935. I was sixteen years old. I was up in Dublin once before. I came up on a half crown[36] excursion to Guiney's. Josie brought us to Dublin. She brought us out to see the sea and she brought us to see the Phoenix Park, two things.

We saw the Wellington Monument in the Phoenix Park, which we thought was terrific, a big, big effort, we thought it was huge. We also went out to Sandymount Strand and we saw the tram there, and we saw the sea. That was the first time I saw the sea. We went back on the train that evening.

There were three ways of coming to Dublin, the train, the Magnet bus and the IOC - the Irish Omnibus Company. It would take two or three hours.

Going to Dublin was like going to Australia. My poor mother was very anxious as to how I was going to get on.

Josie was working in O'Connell's of Parnell Street, a very, very well known grocer's shop and she was on the bacon counter, a good job as jobs went then. The money might not have been good but it was in a very reputable, up-market shop. All white coats and all that. She was living with Rose Casserly, our cousin. Rose was Mary Cunningham's daughter, Aunt Cunney's daughter.

Josie wrote me a letter and told me I was called for an interview and that was the first about it. I was to come up on a given date and I arrived up on that particular date in the middle of the week. I got off the Magnet bus at Church Street Bridge and I went down Church Street to meet Rose Casserley. Josie was expected home for her lunch, she would walk home from O'Connell Street for her lunch. During her lunch hour she took me up to Thomas Street and left me at the Mayo Stores and told me she would see me later. The Mayo Stores was a grocery and provision stores.

I got the start, so I went up to Frawley's of Thomas Street and bought a brown coat and came back and walked in behind the counter in the Mayo Stores with Dan Fox, the

---

[36] A half crown was s2. 6d. Two shillings and sixpence, the equivalent in euro would be 6 cent. The currency values at the time were pounds, shillings and pence (There were twelve pence in a shilling, and twenty shillings in a pound. There was decimalization of the currency in 1970 and pounds and pence became the new values. (There were 100 pence in a pound).

manager of the egg stores. He was from Tyrells Pass. There seemed to be hundreds and thousands of eggs all around, there were boxes and boxes of them.

The boss, Bill, wasn't a very easygoing man; he'd always be sizing you up and down. He called everyone John; it would be a fright if he caught you talking.

I had my tea with the lads in the evening, upstairs over the shop. When we closed the shop in the evening we'd all go upstairs for our tea. I 'lived in' there upstairs over the shop. Paddy Quinn, a Kilbeggan man, I slept with him in one bed, Mick Reynolds from Oldcastle and Jack Murray slept in another bed. Five of us slept in the one room. There were three big double beds in our room. You wouldn't sleep on your own; sure there was a bit of heat in with another fellow. Upstairs on the next floor, there was Tom Molloy from Tullamore, and a brother of his, Ned. There was Paddy Shanley from Enfield, a chap from Kildare and John Kilmurray from Offaly. He was a hard ticket. He would often imitate Bill the boss. There were nine working on the job and they all lived in.

I got four shillings[37] a week. I got paid in an envelope and all. The digs were covered, I didn't pay anything extra.

You got up in the morning at eight of clock; you'd get your breakfast. John's Lane was across the road if you wanted to go to mass. We'd work from half eight until six. There was a cook who would do all the cooking and we were well looked after. In the middle of the day you'd be called up for your dinner, in turn.

There were trams going up and down the road at that time, the tram going out to Inchicore. People would be looking at the tram to see if they knew anybody on it, but it was all new to me. I was just a gábín[38] from the country, but I wasn't long learning. The customers were from all over and around Dublin, it was real Dublin at the time. I must say of the Dublin people, they were people who were not afraid to buy well and eat well, with whatever amount of money they had.

Over the tea in the evening we'd sit and there would be loads of stories, you would be finished work and there would be loads of talk. Then we'd clean up and we'd go out for exercise, a gang of us, five or six of us. We'd walk into town over O'Connell Bridge and then walk up one side of O'Connell Street and then down the other side. The lads might meet somebody that they knew and you'd stand around talking, I didn't know anyone at

---

[37] The equivalent value is 25 cent.
[38] A gábín is a bit of an amateur type of person, or in Dublin slang 'a bit of a thick'.

the time. Anyway we'd walk up and down like that and then come home and be back for ten o'clock to go to bed. Sometimes we'd go out as far as the Bull Wall and walk back again. Or we'd go up the Phoenix Park with a hurley stick, the four of us, Paddy Quinn, Mick Reynolds and Jack Murray.

The fun, the craic and the sport to be had in Dublin

The Esplanade was up the Liffey, up in front of Collins Barracks. Not long after I started in the Mayo Stores there was a big carnival on there for a fortnight. We went up there to see all the various things; there were swing boats and all sorts of boats and two dance halls. The Stratosphere Lady was the big star of the carnival. She climbed up into the stratosphere. She did various tricks, actions and exercises. She looked to be in the heavens; she was so far away. When she was finished her act she would slide down the rope.

We had good fun at the Mayo though. There was great camaraderie. One time I remember going out to Booterstown with the lads. I was known as 'Stormy' cause of the way my hair was off my forehead, with the 'cow's lick'. Well, we went on the tram. All the fellas changed and got into the water. They swam out of course, calling back to me to come out. I wouldn't change till they were well out in the water. I couldn't swim. I thought they would duck me. They were out about fifteen or twenty yards and I decided I'd go for a dip. It was considered a safe place to swim; you could go out a fair bit and still not be out of your depth. I thought it was marvellous being out in the sea in about three and a half feet of water and to be able to float. Well, they came back for 'Stormy'. Well, they got me and ducked me. I swallowed so much water; I cleaned out my system. I nearly choked on the salt water.

The fellas were always playing tricks. Paddy Quinn from Kilbeggan, the chap I used to sleep with, had check trousers, nice material. Paddy would always turn away the sheets and put his trousers in under the sheet. He liked to wear wide legged trousers, a bit wider than the rest of us would wear. He'd dampen the edges of the seams and rub soap along them. He liked to have his trousers really nicely pressed and with a nice crease. Well, one evening, when Paddy went out to the toilet, the lads got the shaving brush and rubbed more soap along the edges all down the seams. Well, when he took them out the next morning, well, there was such an edge on them; you could shave yourself with them. They were so well pressed you couldn't see his shoes. Another night poor Paddy had a date, and he was going out. But instead of finding the trousers pressed, sure the lads had tied the two legs together in a knot, the poor fella, they were all lumpy and crushed.

Paddy would always be out late at night, although you couldn't be out later than eleven 'cause the boss would lock up the house so you wouldn't get in, and you didn't have a key. One of the lads took it upon himself to get a key and it would be thrown out to Paddy at a given time. The boss would be sleeping at the back of the house and you could creep in quietly and he wouldn't know. One of the nights anyhow, the boss happened to be down the house having a few drinks and he found Paddy coming in.

"We keep proper hours in this house, we keep proper hours in this house. Ye will keep proper hours in this place and be in here before eleven and that's the rule".

Well, John Kilmurray answered him back. He told him straight out that he didn't think it mattered what time we got in at as long as we got in before twelve o'clock, and we were down at our job in the morning at half past eight. If we didn't, *then,* there would be something to talk about.

"That's alright," the boss said to John "But I'd don't like it, I don't like it".

It settled down after that.

I didn't go to dances at the beginning, but I did when I got in on the swing of things. I'd go to ceili and old-time. There were two dances you could go to. But you had to be in at eleven o'clock at night in the Mayo.

Dances would be over at half past ten or a quarter to eleven. When I moved away from the Mayo later on, I could stay out as long as I liked. That was just the rule in the Mayo.

For a day's outing you could also get the train out from Harcourt Street to Bray for a shilling and climb Bray Head. I remember the first time I went out on that train, I thought the cliffs would fall, they seemed to be hanging over the train track. The rocks were held back by wire netting, I thought if there was ever a big frost, in the thaw afterwards the rocks would slip down and crush the train. I never fancied that part of the journey.

The smokehouse

We'd have a lot of bacon coming in. It would be all washed in big tanks out the back in the yard. The yard at the back was a big extension properly roofed and very well kept. It was like a huge big bathhouse for washing the bacon. In the big square tanks you'd put four sides of bacon and they would be scrubbed, taken out, wiped off and hung up to dry. That evening they would go into the smokehouse, maybe twenty sides of bacon, we were doing a big trade in the bacon business at the time.

George, the lad who used to smoke the bacon, you'd see him at about four o'clock in the evening going around with a bundle of papers under his arm and a bag of oak sawdust on his way to the smokehouse. The oak sawdust came from the sawmills, it was the genuine article. At this time in the evening the bacon would be hanging in the smokehouse, out of the ceiling, there could be up to thirty sides of bacon and everywhere would be as black as soot, with the ceiling, walls and floor shining black as soot.

George would get down on his two knees and set up a little fire with a bundle of newspapers crushed up, and two or three sods of hard black turf that he'd put standing over the paper and then a good pinch of oak sawdust. He'd go back from time to time to see that his fires were still lighting. He'd have fifteen or twenty of those fires lighting all over the floor of the smokehouse, under the sides of bacon. The smoke in the place would burn the eyes out of you.

The bacon would be smoked overnight. There were always sufficient sides of bacon there for the weekend and we'd have hams hanging in another part of the smokehouse, they would be all hanging up on hooks. The doors of the smokehouse would be left open the following day and a draught created. The bacon would be fairly warm after the smoking overnight, the heat would also help dry out the bacon.

The bacon would be very flexible and soft but if it was smoked and left hanging for a while it would dry out. It would then be taken down and eventually it would be taken out to shop to be sold.

I remember later what I'd often see as smoked bacon. Well, it wouldn't be smoked at all but dyed and left out to dry, it looked like smoked bacon, but people wouldn't be getting the real thing. People would be looking for smoked rashers and when the bacon would be sliced up they mightn't be able to tell the difference but I tell you there would be a big difference in the flavour. Nobody who wanted smoked rashers would ever take pale rashers, pale rashers are white rashers.

I suppose we put up with a lot

There would always be crowds in the shop and three worked in the egg stores and seven in the other section. The boss, he was always following you around the shop. He would often say to someone "Write a letter to your mother so that she won't be surprised when you arrive back home in the yard." He would walk around with his arms folded, I never saw him working but he was always conniving.

I remember one little fella came up from Cavan for a year's experience, he got a lift and came up with an egg lorry.

"They are putting sheep in a pen in O'Connell Street at night so that you fellas won't get lonely" says Bill to him one day, as a bit of 'a joke'.

I suppose people put up with a lot, it was difficult to get a start and there were lots of people looking for work and looking for a job.

'Bill the boss', as we referred to him, was always on the move. You would never know when he would walk up behind your back. He would pretend he was about to walk out of the shop and then he would turn around and say "Oh that reminds me". The first day he did this to me he said "Yes, I have to bring home a pair of chickens today. Yes give me that pair of chickens there at the top of the window. How much are they?"

And I had to sell him the pair of chickens and this is where he would be trying to catch you out. If you dithered at all about it he wouldn't be long telling you "See 'tis this like this John", he called everyone John as I said "You'll have to smarten up a bit cause the customer is waiting for the pair of chickens". I was trying to sell him the chickens. "You'll have to be quicker, speed, speed all the time". "I understand that" I said. "But that won't do" said Bill.

Another day he came into the shop to do something similar. He had come in from the smokehouse with a paper in his hand and he looked along the counter. "Mmmm you have eggs in the window, I see you have eggs there today, I see they are eleven pence a dozen. Well, I would like some for my wife for baking. How many would I get for ten pence?" I told him and he paused. "Have you better value than that? A bit of discussion followed. And then he said "Well, 'tis like this John, 'tis like this, you see I'm only just saying, there are a lot of customers around here and they are all in a bit of a hurry and they don't like you to keep them waiting. Keep moving, keep moving, there are no stationary places".

I suppose I was always a bit casual and I suppose half a citog[39] I used my left hand and my right hand. One particular day, I wasn't long in the place, and Bill the boss came in behind my back. "What happened your other arm?" says he, "Is it broken?" or something to that effect. "No" says I, "I'm in the habit of using my left hand"

"Your left hand? Well, do you use your left hand all the time?"

"Well, not all the time"

"Well, you want to do something about that now John. I am a long time in the business and, well… I've never employed a left-handed man in my life, 'cause we've no left handed machines and we've no left-handed this and no left-handed that".

---

[39] A left-handed person.

Well, I got a bit of a shock. And then he says "Well, you better keep in touch with your mother anyway 'cause she might be seeing you someday." I knew he said that to everyone, but he'd be half serious about it. You'd be hoping that when a Saturday night came there would be only one week's wages there, not two. If there were two, you were a goner.

Well, after that episode with Bill all the lads were at me when we went up for the dinner. "Lynam, you're an awful bloody man, why didn't you use your right hand and put your left hand away when he was watching you?" I said I didn't know. "Well, you know now and that's what he will be watching for." From there on in, I made sure I didn't make much use of my left hand. At dinner time there might be five or six of us around the table and someone would ask me to pass the butter. If I didn't pass with the right hand and I used my left hand, the knuckles were nearly cut off me by one of the fellas. "Use your bloody right hand". Anyway with that sort of practice it was about a fortnight after that I could say to myself "I think I'm good enough now to be able to use my two hands".

I didn't write with my left hand, I never did at school. I could never make a job of writing with my left hand. When I was playing football I'd always played best with my left foot. Sure I was all upset. But I could share work with both hands.

I wasn't long in the Mayo, and I suppose I was a bit lonely. All the fellas were all going off to Rathfarnham Castle on a weekend retreat, well, they were going off on the Saturday evening at six o'clock and would be back on the Monday morning. It was normal at that time for fellas to go off once a year on retreat, all on their bikes. The lads told me all about it. Well, I knew I wasn't on the retreat list, but I thought I'd get a chance to go if I got the OK from Bill. So I asked Bill on the Saturday that they were going off.
"Excuse me sir, I was just wondering if I could go off with the lads on the retreat?" and I explained about all the lads going off after work.
"That's right, that's right… Retreat… mm… Well," and he paused another bit. "Not tonight… You can go next year with them when they are going" and he turned and walked away.
After a few feet, he turned half around and said "Well, that is if you are still here, do you see, that is if you are still here" As much as to say whatever might have been the chance of you going tonight, you mightn't have a chance of going next year … 'cause there was a chance that you wouldn't be there.

I didn't go then or maybe the following year, but to think now that I have been actively promoting and have organised retreats every year for the past… well, I started in 1964 and I had a great crowd again this year, Thank God. What's that? Forty years?

I remember fellas coming and going from the Mayo. They would come up and arrive in the morning and be gone home in the evening 'cause they wouldn't take any nonsense from Bill the boss. I suppose they hadn't got to take it from him, but I was just the poor old Joe Soap up from the country and I had to make the best of it. "You're up from the country do you see" Bill would always remind you. Fellas would change their pattern in life. There was one chap in the Mayo for about a year. I met him on the road one time going through Enfield on my way home to Mullingar. He had an ass and cartload of turf bringing it home from the bog, I think near his parent's place. "Imagine meeting you out here". We had a great old chat and talked about the Mayo. It might have been the best thing he'd ever done leaving the Mayo, he might have chosen to go on later to bigger and better things. You never know what's at the other side of the road for you, 'till you cross it.

Keeping in contact with home

If you went for a stroll down O'Connell Street, you'd always see fellas going in and out of the GPO to drop a line home. You'd buy your notepaper and envelopes in Woolworth's, you would get all you needed for a few coppers. The post office was very convenient, you got your stamp there and there were prepared tables where there was ink and pens –end pens, they had a wooden handle with a metal nib at the end. There'd be two fellas at one end of the table and another two along the other end, writing. There was a saying 'never buy ink while there's a post office in town'. You'd stand up at the tables to write, the tables were high up against the wall. You could write your letter there with your back to the rest of the people in the post office. You would get your stamp from the girl at the counter, you would post it in the pillar-box and your mother would have the letter by the weekend.

My mother would never cease to write. She would always write. She would give you all the news about whatever was happening at home, and about the locals. I did write back with whatever bit of news I had. I would write a letter once a week. You were working in Dublin and that was it. They had their life to live and I had my life to live as it were.

Apart from the working time and the working life, which I spent with the lads, I had lots of free time. I'd see Josie in the course of the week and if ever we had occasion or the need to talk about something. I also could spend time with some of my cousins, the Cunninghams, in Dublin, they lived in different places around Dublin. Bill Cunningham, one of the cousins, was living out in Clontarf. He was milking sixty-two cows then, in stables and cowsheds, in Vernon Avenue, Clontarf. The first time I ever saw a big plate of lettuce, with all the ingredients for a salad, was in that house. There was a big bowl, like a big basin, in the middle of the table, when it was empty; everyone could leave the table.

As I was saying, I was living 'indoor' when I came to town, and the wages I was getting was little or nothing. I couldn't afford to send money home. You could barely get by. I was supported from home, my mother would send me pocket money on and off. I would never have enough of money to send money home, and I couldn't afford to go home. I saved for six months to go home the first Christmas. I had Christmas Day and Stephen's Day. Then we got five days' holiday in the year and an extra half-day if you were travelling. You worked a six-day week.

I was a bad traveller. Of course, on the bus, I wasn't the only one; there were others like me. You'd keep in touch with the conductor. If you felt like getting sick the bus would stop for you. You could walk around the back of the bus and get a bit of air.

You could always be let go from a job

People worked hard in those days. If you were working in an office, or doing books, at the end of the day if the money was out even one penny, you wouldn't be allowed put the penny in. You had to go over and over the books and the cash till you found out where the mistake was, then you could go home for the evening. And you never knew really when you might be let go. You could just be told there wasn't enough work for you.

There were different ways too that people were tested. You could get a start on a Monday and be let go on a Saturday and just be told you weren't suitable. There was one story about how one boss used to test a fellow's honesty. He'd start someone on a Monday, say a messenger boy, and on Saturday evening the lad would be told to sweep up the floor. The floor was covered in sawdust and the boss would put an old English threepenny bit[40] into the sawdust. If the young lad handed up the threepence he was kept on.

Working in Chatham Street

My second job was in Kelly's of Chatham Street. Over the door it said '*Kelly's, Late of Leveret and Fry*'. The boss was a foreman in Leveret and Fry before he opened his own shop, which was only across the road from Leveret and Fry. Mrs Kelly was in charge of the shop when I was there, her husband wasn't too well at the time.

It was an up-market shop. People would arrive early in the morning, pull up in a Ford driven car, leather gloves, all that type of thing, all ladies, veterinary surgeons' wives, all that sort of people, nice people. The chauffeur would park the car in Chatham Street.

---

[40] An English threepenny bit was a gold coloured coin.

Madame would come in and leave her order and then go off shopping in Grafton Street. The chauffeur would call later and collect the order. Generally, the ladies went to Bewley's for coffee. You'd see them coming back, the chauffeur opening the door for them and they sitting in - very lady-like people - and off they would go home. They always wanted very good quality food. They wouldn't buy a lot. They would call into us and buy something small, whatever was on the menu that day. A poor person would spend their week's wages on a basket of food and they would have enough for three or four days. These people would buy fresh food everyday. It seemed they liked to get out in the morning to go strolling and shopping in Grafton Street.

Justice Kingsley Moore's wife was a customer of ours, a lovely person. Liam Cosgrove's grandmother was also a customer. There were two lads, another and myself, and two messengers on messenger bikes for people who wanted their order delivered. There were lots of deliveries to Aylesbury Road.

At this time I was staying in Church Street. Before I would go to work, I would walk to the Dublin Corporation market, buy the fresh fruit and vegetables, or whatever else that would be needed and then head over to Grafton Street. I would leave the stuff with Boggan's, and the messenger would go over later to collect it and bring it back on the carrier bike.

For recreation there was always the football and the hurling

As I was saying, when I came to town first I got little or no wages, and I couldn't afford to go home. But I'd always find recreation for myself along with other lads. We'd always go to cheap football matches.

When I came to town first, I was able to go to Croke Park three times in the one day. You'd start off in the morning, probably at a club match. These matches started at a quarter to twelve in the morning. The reason why they were at that time was there was a tremendous number of barmen who played the matches, and they would have to be into work at half past one. Then I'd go home to the digs for the dinner; we had our dinner in the middle of the day then.

The next match would be at a quarter to two, or two fifteen or half two. It wasn't far from where I was staying, about a mile. After I moved from the Mayo Stores I moved into digs with Mrs Behan in Church Street. I'd walk down to Croke Park and queue up at the boy's gate. I would be a bit tall at the boy's gate. You'd have to have your knees working well. You'd lower your height a bit. They would be busy and they wouldn't be taking too much notice and you'd hand in, I think it was sixpence at the time, that you had to pay into senior matches. You'd pay your sixpence and got in, not on the sideline but amongst the general public. You'd keep rooting away till you were probably up against the railings. There was nobody putting you in your place or anything like that. There were no stewards then; you just stood around wherever. 'Hill 16' was always a great place. It was on a fall of ground and I was tall. You could always follow the matches. At that time an All Ireland Programme was 2d. (two pence). I have several of them still. I know more about the hurlers from Cork and Limerick. It was great recreation altogether.

I was always interested in hurling as a child, more so than football. I played around at home out in the fields along with the rest of the lads, my brothers. I wasn't an expert, but I knew about hurling. I knew all the famous men who played hurling. You'd look up to them; they were top class hurlers. You wouldn't be on speaking conditions with them, but you knew all about them. Its like the soccer crowd today, with big heroes. It was great.

When the matches would be over at the end of the day, you'd stand around talking about the match, discussing what you thought of the team, what you thought of the game. I would be on my own, but when you would come out of Croke Park and stand along the footpath you'd see all the people coming out. You'd surely see someone you knew from the country, or from somewhere else. If there were people up from home, after the match you'd know you would meet up with them at a particular spot on the road. That was the meeting place and sure we all knew it.

The days you wouldn't be going to Croke Park you would go up to the Phoenix Park with your hurley stick. You'd spend the morning hurling above in the Phoenix Park just playing around and then you'd go home for your dinner at one o'clock. There were always people up there like myself, keen to play. There'd be a line of people, five or six, along a stretch of ground - alongside one of the hurling grounds. There might be a match on, or fellas might be there practising. If you had your hurley stick you'd get in on the end. Any ball that would go loose, you'd go over and pick it up and hit it back to the lads. When the others would discover that you were keen to play ball like themselves, they would take you in and you'd get to know them and then you were part of the lads. You'd never be short of someone to play with; there were always loads of others. At that time I was still only breaking into Dublin life.

Sometime later, I joined O'Raghallaigh's Hurling Club, and later again I joined St. Colmcille's Hurling Club.

Wearing a path to the Mail office looking for jobs

You would be always wondering about the job you were in, and if there might be a chance to get a better one, it wasn't easy to change jobs. You'd jump at any chance to go for an interview. You wouldn't be buying the newspaper and you'd have a path worn out going to the Evening Mail office to see what adds were in the paper and to see if there was anything at all that suited you. If there was anything going you would leave in your replies to the advertisements to the post office box number. Or you would send off your application in the post. You would wait and people might, or they might not, get back to you. You would put your own add in too. "Farmer's son looking for work" was always a popular one. You would pay your money for your add and you would be given a ticket with a number. You would go in everyday to see if there were any replies to your add. You would hand in your ticket and the woman behind the counter would go to the pigeonhole with your number. You might see a few envelopes and hope that they were in your slot. There would be loads of people going in and out of the Mail.

Jobs and work were very scarce and you were working for buttons. And you were very glad to get the buttons, 'cause people would take anything they could to be working at all.

I remember I went for one job as a sweet boiler in Dun Laoghaire, to NKM - North Kerry Manufacturers. They made caramel sweets. I went out on the train for that, but they were looking for apprentices and that didn't suit me. There was another job as a hairdresser in High Street, but you had to work on Sunday and I wasn't interested in that.

LEINSTER SENIOR FOOTBALL FINAL.

KILDARE

v.

LOUTH

AT

CROKE PARK,

ON

SUNDAY, 28th. JULY 1935,

STARTING AT 3-30.

Programme

Up for the All Ireland 1936. Pat, Bill, Tom and Mick Ryan on O' Connell Bridge.

Bill and Mary up at the orchard gate.

(L-R) Maureen Murray, Rita Cox, Mother, Annie Murray.

Preparing for the turf cutting 1936, aged 17, on my summer holidays.

Bringing home the turf during the holidays, 1936.

Catching turf. (L-R) Peter Rourke, Jim, Tom.

Top to bottom. Pat, Mick Ryan, Tom, building a haggard cock of hay, 1937.

Pat swarth turning.

Bringing home the hay on the boogey.

Pat, Tom and Lilly Cunningham dressed for a bit of lark, 1939.

Lilly Cunningham, with sweet fingers feeding calves at the
top of the yard in Marlinstown, on holidays in 1938.

Maureen O' Sullivan, a friend from Hull in 1939.

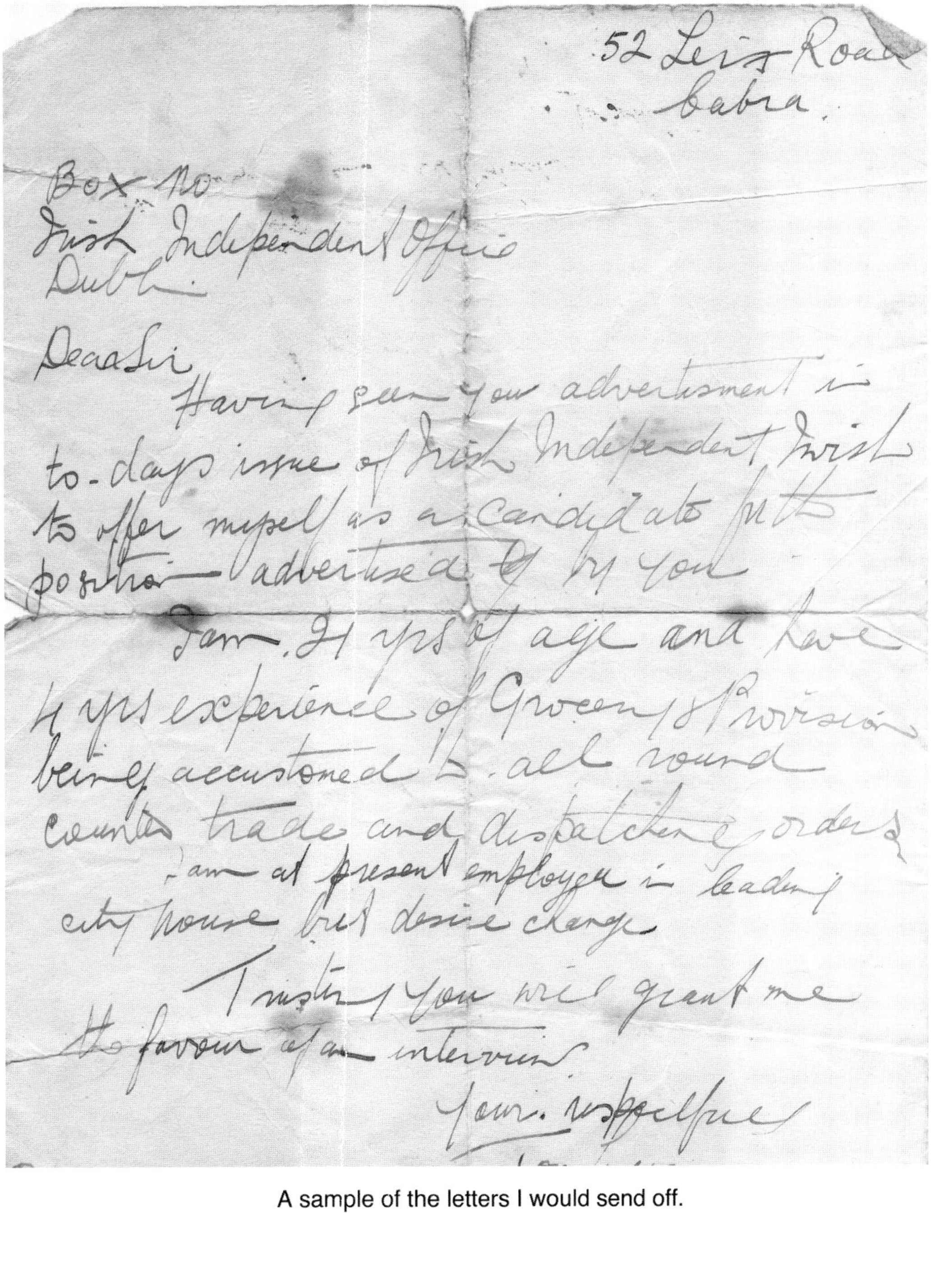

52 Leix Road
Cabra.

Box No
Irish Independent Office
Dublin

Dear Sir
Having seen your advertisment in
to-days issue of Irish Independent, I wish
to offer myself as a candidate for the
position advertised by you

I am 21 yrs of age and have
4 yrs experience of Grocery & Provision
being accustomed to all round
counter trade and dispatching orders
I am at present employed in leading
city house but desire change.

Trusting you will grant me
the favour of an interview.

Yours respectfully

A sample of the letters I would send off.

Uncle Tom and Jack, rolling the wooden iron shod cart wheels into the 'Kills' pond. In very hot weather it was neccessary to swell the wood and tighten the grip of the iron.

Pat and Grandfather Matt Loughrey in Marlinstown in 1939.

The house at home.

Established 1823

TELEGRAPHIC ADDRESS "WINE" DUBLIN.
TELEPHONE Nº— 44317 (4 LINES)

Alex Findlater & Co Ltd
Findlater's Corner
28, 29, 30, 31 & 32, Upper O'Connell St.
Dublin c.8

GDF/LC.

22nd. Feb. 1939.

Thomas Lynam Esq.
52 Leix Road,
CABRA.
Dublin.

Dear Sir,

    We are in receipt of your application of the 22nd. inst.
but regret we have no vacancy in our Company at the moment.
We are filing your application for future reference and should
a suitable vacancy occur, we will get in touch with you.

       Yours faithfully,

ALEX FINDLATER & Co., Ltd.

A sample of a reply you would receive.

"When can you start?" - the day for me that it all began

I was so happy the day I got the job in the Coombe. The way it happened was that I was at a party one night. It was a big hooley[41] out in Finglas in my cousins' house, the Cunninghams. They knew lots of people, barmen, people working in town and all with an interest or involved in football and hurling. I would have been like the junior person of that gang at the time. I knew the cousins well, I would go out there on my half-day and do the garden for them and I would be around for the craic, and I would have been looked after, and have the evening meal with them. On this particular night there was a man there, Joe Swan was his name. He worked for K & S Sunshine Works. My cousin Rose Casserley, that I was in digs with in Cabra, got talking to him. On the Monday after the hooley she made enquiries about any jobs that might be going, she explained to him that her cousin Tom was anxious to move jobs, not that there was a problem with where he was but that there wasn't really a future there for him. He suggested that I go over to Pidgeons in the Coombe on the Tuesday. That was all the information I needed.

On Tuesday at my lunch break, I went over to the Coombe to meet Mr Cowley who owned Pidgeons. Lillian Byrne, who was in charge of the office, asked me to hold on a minute, Mr Cowley would be soon back from his lunch. I didn't want to stay 'cause it was against my principles to be back to work late from lunch. He finally turned up. I asked about the possibility of a job in the new shop in Cabra and explained that I really wanted to work, but I couldn't see any prospects for improvement where I was at the moment. After another bit of discussion he said that it was all women that they employed in the Coombe. I saw that myself when I was waiting, there were about eight girls behind a very long and busy bacon counter, with loads and loads of bacon and plenty of work. I told him I wouldn't mind taking a girl's job, because I'd take anything to get a chance.
"Well" he said, "you are very anxious." Then he said, "Well, if we were to give you a job, when could you start?"
I nearly had a seizure when he said, "When could you start?" I told him I would have to give notice. I knew that was very important to give a good account of yourself. If you were in a job and you walked out of it and left it and it didn't work for you, people would be saying you couldn't have much luck anyway for letting the other woman down or that man down. I wasn't prepared to do that. Mr Cowley told me to do whatever I needed to do and to come and join them as soon as I could; he would like to take me on.

I gave notice to the shop in Chatham Street. Mrs Kelly said, "Certainly Thomas, if you think it is going to improve your prospects, I will do nothing to stand in your way, I'll help you in whatever way I can". I was happy with what I was doing. I rang Pidgeons and told

---

[41] A party, a get-together.

them I would start on Monday morning. I had been three and a half years in Dublin; I was twenty years of age.

The first meeting with the Lovely Rose from Clare

I arrived over on the Monday morning in the Coombe. When I got to the shop, there was nobody there; I was the first to arrive. There was no sight of this other person who was supposed to take up the job. Next thing she came cycling on her bicycle up into the yard in the back. She had long dark curly hair and was wearing a spotlessly clean white shop coat. She looked full of beans. She was only in the shop for twenty minutes or so. Mr Cowley spoke with her. She must have been told that there was a change of plan and that there was a man in the shop that had been taken on, and that she would be starting in the new shop in Cabra instead. She was given directions to the new shop in Cabra, where she was now going to start. She really left an impression on me.

Treasa had worked in the Pioneer Stores in Inchicore and she had a contact to the Coombe and that's how she had been recommended. She was to be taken on as extra staff in the Coombe 'cause I think some of the Coombe staff were to be moved over to Cabra with the opening of the new shop in the following few days. I suppose Treasa was the one that got shifted. She used to joke and say that she was under the impression all her life that I took her job. But I remember her so well, as I said, full of beans, that first day that I saw her.

Taking a girl's job, the best way to a bright future

I was now in the Coombe and the first thing that I wondered was, "What in God's name do they do with all the food?" There was more food there, than you would sell in Chatham Street in a month, well, in a week anyway. I was the only man amongst women and I could see nothing but work all around me and I was charmed to see that. We had all electric slicers, which I wasn't familiar with using, and I thought this was great.

Well, one day borrowed another, I was appreciated and I was getting on great. The first week I thanked the girl behind the counter that was responsible for getting me to wait that lunchtime I came over to meet the boss. Then the money came round and everyone got their wages. But I got no wages. I wondered, and I spoke to Lillian in the office.
"Thomas" says she, "I'll have a word with him tomorrow."

Well, he came over to me in the middle of the following week and apologised for that happening. I said it was alright, I understood, there was probably an error somewhere. I had already told him, when I first met him, that I would work for a girl's wages. Girls were getting £2.10.00 a week.[42]

"I could not have anyone working behind my counter for two pounds and ten shillings a week, I couldn't offer that to any man." he said. "We will start you off on £4.[43] Tell Lillian to give you four pounds."

Well, I got four pounds as against two pounds and ten shillings that the others, all girls, were earning.[44] I was about twenty years of age at the time. They were the same age as me, all late teenagers or early twenties. There was nobody older than that. In the factory there were a few married women.

I thought Mr Cowley must have liked me. I could see nothing else but that he liked me. I was getting on with everyone; everyone seemed to like me. As time went on things got even better. Mr Cowley owned the Pidgeons' shops, seven of them. A Westmeath man, from Ballinagore, Tom Cowley was his name. A good family man, he had three daughters and a young son, and they were often in and around the shop. The boss and I got on very well, 'cause all I wanted to do was get into work after a very, very, very, quiet, easy time in Chatham Street, well, it wasn't easy for me, 'cause I was looking for *work*.

An introduction to the Vincent de Paul and the Legion

One day, I was about six months or more working in the Coombe and Mr Cowley asked me if I was doing anything that night.
"Why?" I asked, "Is there something on?"
"No" he said, "I was just thought you might like to come up to Francis Street, to join the Vincent de Paul Society 'cause you seem like the right type of person for it."
"Oh thanks very much" I said, "But I don't know about that."
"Come up" he said, "I'm President of one of the Conferences up there."

So I found myself up in Francis Street[45] with Vincent de Paul fellas all around the place, all nice fellas, I didn't really know what it was all about but I decided to stay. I enjoyed every

---

[42] The current equivalent value is €3.17.

[43] Current equivalent value is €5.8.

[44] Equal Pay for equal work was legislated for under a European Economic Community Directive in 1973 after Ireland joined the European Common Market in 1972. However, research has shown that women in Ireland in 2003, still earn up to 30% less than their male counterparts, even in the high tech industries.

[45] The Vincent de Paul Conferences met in 100 Francis Street in Myra House, a centre of The Legion of Mary. 'The Legion' was founded by Dubliner Frank Duff. It was born out of concern for the spiritual needs of the poor of the Liberties area. One of the earliest endeavours was to close the brothels in the Monto, in the North Inner City in 1925. Frank Duff was also a member of the Vincent de Paul, which used Myra House free of charge for many years.

moment of it, what an experience working with the Vincent de Paul. And then I lined up with my friend Tom McSweeney. More on that later.

People ask, "How did you ever get into things?" Well, one Saturday the boss Tom Cowley asked me if I would do him a favour. He told me that the Legion of Mary was running an outing out to Donabate, Frank Duff and the whole lot were going.
"There is a big order in there. Jimmy McKeown is bringing it out, but I would like you to see that everything is alright 'cause I took it on myself to do this and I know you could take my place." I said I'd have a go at it.

So off I went out to Donabate and I took part in everything in it. There were three-legged races with women I never saw before and all sorts of things, great craic. That evening I was walking up Parnell Square, I got a lift back in one of the vans and this man began to ask me how I got involved in the Legion of Mary?
Says I "I'm not involved in the Legion at all."
"And how did you get out to Donabate on a Legion outing?"
"Well, Tom Cowley sent me out to see that you were all happy and got plenty to eat, I went out with the lad in the van, and now I'm home with you people."
"Well, what are you doing on Wednesday evening? I have a Presidium, which in the Legion is the same as a Conference, over there in Fosses, at the back of Parnell Square. We have a meeting on Wednesday, will you come and join us?"

Well, I joined the Legion that evening, that's how I joined it. It wasn't long till I was serving my time to it, and I was up to my ears in it. I was everywhere with the Legion from Lough Derg, to - you name it. I was at various outings with the Legion of Mary with Frank Duff, and Herbert Niall. My boss Tom Cowley was a big figure in the Legion.

Pidgeons in the Coombe, the counter, food and much more

Pidgeons also had a factory up in Coombe Street. There was about eight or ten girls working up in the factory. The butchers up there prepared the sausages. They would send the sausages over to us in a bath, about forty or fifty pounds of sausages at a time. They would come in loose lines. We would take them in lengths and hang them on hooks, and then hang the sausages along, like curtains, on an iron bar. There were big dishes of black and white pudding; we had pigs' heads, cowheel, tripe. We had rashers to beat the band. We had back rashers, streaky rashers, narrow back rashers, wide back rashers, and collar rashers for coddle.[46]

---

[46] Coddle is a Dublin dish, a type of stew made with potatoes, a few coddling rashers, a few sausages, an onion, and some thyme and lots of water. It would be left cooking for up to four hours. When it is infused

We had a section where we sold rabbits that would come in from the trappers; the rabbits were trapped up in Co. Wicklow. Tuesday was always rabbit day. I would have a pain in my face cutting out one-and a-half-pound pieces of streaky bacon. People would ask for 'one-and-a-half-pounds'. Well, the one-and-a-half-pound piece of streaky bacon and a rabbit was a small family dinner. The demand for that was great. They might take one or two or more rabbits and bacon pieces, depending on the size of the family. It went like hot cakes.

We all worked on cash registers and the registers were counted every evening before we left. And life went on.

We sold a lot of food. Before I went to work in the Coombe, I was very ignorant, and for the first two days that I was there, I wondered what the people did with all the food. I wondered if they had little guesthouses or something. "Are you codding us, those people will be back again before tea-time for more."

Now the people in the Liberties could eat and they always fed themselves well. It was such a different experience to Chatham Street. Still today I meet people that I served in the Coombe at the Punchestown Races or at the Galway Races, they are still selling apples and oranges and bars of chocolate off trays, after the second last and the last race.
And when I meet them. "How are you Josephine?"
"Ah is it you Lynam down here?"

And they leave down the oranges they are selling and throw their arms around me. Those were the people I worked with in the Coombe, the decentest people ever. This year in Galway I met Josie again, still travelling and selling with her stall at eighty-nine years of age and still full of life and fresh looking.

There might be the odd one, that might have come out of prison after doing a week or two for taking a bit of drapery up in Thomas Street or somewhere else. But that would be forgotten and would be all over. But then our own customers, who would be in three times a day, would warn you.

---

and holds the flavours of the contents of the coddle, the liquid makes a lovely 'gravy' and you can have 'your dinner poured out'.

"Lynam watch out, such and such is out today and they might be trying to get their dinner off you. She'll come in, she'll do you, and she'll try to get her dinner off you if you are not careful."

I got on very well and I was a happy man. Dublin was a very friendly place then. And I was very much involved in social activity; there was no such thing as idle time. We were very privileged. The customers were the best. They would be two deep in the shop. If you went to serve a woman that you thought might only want something little, you'd hear "Keep your eyes off the women with the fancy clothes, don't forget the shawlies". They always had a great wit. So many of them were on the stage in the old Theatre Royal, great people. Life was hard and all go and I can safely say that I loved every minute of it.

There were horses all around the city. There was no other transport. In the wintertime especially, you'd hear cries of "Coal blocks, blocks, blocks, coal blocks" from the fellas selling blocks of wood. People were very kind to their horses. They kept them in the backyards of houses, in yards all around the Coombe, and over in Smithfield.

Kevin Street Garda Station was just down the road from the Coombe. We were close to the station. The lads would be going in at about half past nine for a cup of tea, after being out on the beat from six in the morning. They'd come in to buy a rasher or a sausage and then go back and cook up a bit of a breakfast in the mess in the station. They would go out from the base on particular duties after that, and we'd meet them in the course of the morning and we'd chat them. We had nicknames on them all. That's when I got to know Jim Hennelly first, he was a gársún[47] in Kevin Street garda station, like the other few junior garda who had been sent up to Dublin. Months later I saw him on duty outside Croke Park, I think he was stationed in Fitzgibbon Street then. But the real story is that years later I met Jim at a parent teacher meeting in James Street. We got talking anyway about how we got there.
"My young fella goes here",
"So does mine".
"What's your lad's name?"
"Justin",
"Well, my lad's name is Ciarán and the two of them are the best of pals. I think we are ringing a bell here".
I can't remember how many years had passed since I had last seen him. And sure then we ended up living on the Drive.

---

[47] Gársún is the Irish word for 'a young fella'.

There were times I could eat out of the boss's pocket. I was never too big that I couldn't do that something little extra. I was always there to help out, at all times. That's the way I always worked. Mr. Cowley was a decent man. He was also interested in hurling. I remember one evening after we tidied up Mr Cowley asking me what I was doing after work.

"There's a couple of hurley sticks in the back of the car, I was wondering if you would come up to the Park if you are not starving for your tea?"

There was a Scribben's on the shelf. A Scribben's was a large round jam-sandwich sponge with cream in the middle, made by Scribben's, who were confectioners in Marrowbone Lane. He took down the Scribben's off the shelf and broke it in two and gave me half of it. "That will keep us going till we get our tea," says he.

And off we went with the hurley sticks to the park and we hurled around for about an hour and then he left me home. That's the type of relationship I had with the boss. Another evening there was stuff coming in from Hanley's of Rooskey and he asked me if I could stay back and take it in. "I'll relieve you another evening, I have to go to a Legion of Mary meeting".

He was easy going; his wife was a bit particular and very refined. She often said that he was a bit clotty in the house. She would say that to the girls. She said that she would find his trousers in the morning and she'd wonder which leg he took out of them last, in other words, he would drop them on the floor when he took them off rather than fold them and put them away. But they got on very well the pair of them.

Pidgeons and pigs

We would be killing twenty pigs a week, at least that many. There was a big demand in pigs' cheeks. The pig's head would be cut off the carcass, then be split in two halves with an eye on both sides, naturally. The split head would have a section of brains on both sides. You would take the brains out; they were thrown away in a bucket. The head was severed and cut off below the jowl, that's the soft fleshy bit under the chin. There was a good lump of meat in the jowl. You would cut it off, and put the jowl into salt to cure it. The half pig's cheek would then be put into a barrel. You couldn't use a pig's cheek unless a great portion of the jowl was taken away, and that you had left it only with the leaner part. When the half heads were cured they were sold as pigs' cheeks.

The jowl part was packed away in boxes or in a barrel, in coarse salt, and it was left there. It would be changed from one box to another, taken out of one box and put into another in fresh coarse salt, until it was well matured in the salt. You could then use it as bacon effect, as back bacon or whatever. Or you could boil it, and you could use it as boiled cheek, it would be very fat though. There was a time when there was very little meat of any sort available in shops and there was great sale in it. We used to call it 'fat ends' or 'cheek ends'. People outside Dublin, in the country were always looking for it, we'd send it down in sections, in five or six or eight pound parcels. We'd send it through the post to people in the country and they would use it for boiled bacon and cabbage. It was never greatly in demand though. The big demand was in pigs' cheeks.

We never sent the jowl to England; it never left the country. There was another part of the jowl that we used, when it was in pork form, before it was cured, the fatty part. We would have it chopped up into very small pieces of fat, and it would go into sausages. Jowl would be used in the making of black pudding too. At that time you might often see in good black pudding, little spots or squares of white fat like the size of peas. It would be mixed into the blood with the other things that went into the making of black pudding, onions, pimento and salt. The little bits of pig's jowl would be sufficient to give it that extra bit of flavour. Today black pudding would have blood and flavourings, but good black pudding then would have little bits of fat running through it.

Pigs were bought at the market on the North Circular Road, at the place known as the Cattle Market. On cattle market mornings, it was a very busy place. Men, drovers, would drive cattle to the market and they would walk from as far as Meath. You'd see all the drovers standing at Hanlon's Corner. The men would be waiting for work, for a chance to be called to drive cattle for all those English people, buyers, who would have bought cattle at the market that morning and who would need them driven down to the North Wall to the boat, to be taken to England that evening. The North Circular Road, Prussia Street all around there would be full of cattle. There was a great export of live cattle. The cattle boats wouldn't only take cattle. An awful lot of people travelled to England on the cattle boats looking for work, the cattle would be in the base of the boats, the people on top looking down on them.

I remember when the boss was on holidays I would sometimes go to buy the pigs at the market. I'd pick out the pigs that I thought would suit us in the pork trade. I'd want about twenty pigs. That would be enough for us for the week. I would have had the pigs bought by nine o'clock in the morning; the sale of pigs would be over early. I then had to mark the pigs. The way we did that, well, it was a delicate job, you'd have to put our mark on the pig's hip, scrape it on the skin on the hip with a blade, a little scut of a penknife. I can't remember if it was an x or 'P' for Pidgeons. You would have to be very careful not to cut the skin and make the pig bleed. I remember one morning; I got a bit of a start. I went a bit heavy on the marker and I could see the blood coming. I quickly got the pigs out on the road and got them up to the abattoir. We used to have the pigs killed in the abattoir off the North Circular, across the road from the cattle market. But nobody ever passed a remark. It wouldn't be very nice if anyone saw blood on the pig's hip. I wasn't in the habit of doing it.

In the evening we'd send down a truck or two trucks to collect the pigs from the abattoir and then they would be butchered. They'd end up as the bacon, rashers and sausages that the people enjoyed eating. We used to say "We buy pigs and the only thing we let away is the squeal". We couldn't harness the squeal.

Joe Shine was one of the bosses. He normally bought the pigs; I went with him on a few occasions to see how things were done.

Going to Dances and Ceili and Old-time

There was a ceili in the Mansion House, and it would finish at half ten, there was a dance in the Teachers that finished at eleven – that was at the other side of the town and then on the other side of Parnell Square, there was ceili and old-time run by the Leeside at Barry's Hotel, and that was over at a quarter past twelve. So you could actually be at three dances in the one night. We only paid into the ceili at the Mansion House. The others we'd arrive into late. We'd know the fellas on the door, and we didn't pay in there – you'd just give them the nod. We'd have a half-hour's dancing in the Teachers and then nearly an hour in Barry's. We got to know people in all those places. Tom McSweeney was mad for the dancing too.

We'd usually finish up a night's dancing by going over to the Mullingar Dairy on Parnell Street for a pint of milk and a shinguard. A shinguard was an apple tart or an apple pastry shaped like the back of your hand. You could have it hot or cold, but it was generally served hot out of the oven. On an evening when there would be no dances, you could often go for a walk out to the Bull Wall, that would be about two miles out on the Clontarf side of the city.

Making music on Howth Head

I had a friend Sean Penston, from Wexford, a barman. He played the squeezebox, the accordion. He wasn't in the Vincent de Paul; he was a shade of that group. We sometimes used to unite over a game of cards on a Sunday afternoon or that, and we might arrange to go out to Howth on the tram during the week. Or we might go out on a Sunday evening if it was fine; the pubs were closed on a Sunday evening. Sean would always bring 'the box'.

We would generally hit up with a decent tram conductor. He'd be going around "Fares please! Fares please." He'd come to us and say, "OK lads, the gentleman downstairs paid for you"

"Which one?"

"The gentleman with the hard hat.... So you're OK".

He would give us the nod and we didn't have to pay. He'd move on to the next seat "Fares now please! Fares now please!". When we'd be getting off the tram he'd say "I hope you enjoy your evening on the Head, see you on the way back." That sort of thing.

We'd pause around for a while and then we might think of having a bit of music. We'd look around for three or four rocks together on a rocky face where it might be comfortable to sit down. We'd roll up our coats and sit off there, and Sean would begin playing away. We'd have great craic and of course we'd also enjoy the comments and the compliments of the people passing by. We'd gather up whatever bits and pieces we had and head off home in the light, at about nine or ten.

We used to have a card school in Sean's digs in Cunningham's in Glasnevin. They lived on St. Teresa's Road, in number eight. At about nine o'clock on a Sunday evening, there might be about ten people there. The landlady would be playing cards with the rest of us and before we'd leave we were always sure of getting a cup of tea. We'd play the ordinary customary 'fifteen' or 'twenty-five'. Then, if on a night there were only two or three people there, we would have a nice bit of chat.

Working with the Vincent de Paul taught me a lot

As I said, I was no length working in the Coombe until I got so much involved, in Catholic action, if you like, in the Vincent de Paul first and then in the Legion of Mary. The Legion had always activities on a Sunday that you would have to attend to. There were so many outings and activities on a Sunday; plenty of functions and your time was so.... Well, you just didn't have enough time. You would meet so many people and that would be the success in it.

I don't know at what stage, or how I got in with Tom McSweeney. He was from Limerick, he was a draper's assistant and we became great friends. He was very much in Colmcille's Hurling Club. I just don't know now, how I first came in contact with him, but I do know he was one honourable fellow. We were best pals, we cycled the country together, went anywhere and everywhere ... and to every sort of match. I joined his club, St Colmcilles.

Then I got Tom McSweeney involved in the Vincent de Paul and he was glad of it. We had a great time and a very enjoyable time with the Vincent de Paul. There was plenty of work to do, going around doing visitation, going around visiting old people or visiting people living on the clippings of tin.... And no money at all. If we thought they were worthy we would make a case for them to receive support from the Vincent de Paul. We thought we were marvellous - we could arrange with them to give them a voucher of three shillings and sixpence[48] to a family - that's the sort of poverty there was around. I was twenty years of age then. Sure you were very young at twenty at that time, they are grown men now at twenty. We visited families, many families at the time.

The people that wanted help would write to our Conference. People could be referred too, normally we got a list of referrals through Francis Street Parish and they would be sent just across the road to Myra House.[49]

We were living on the Northside and we worked on the Southside. I'm not sure why it was done like that, but that was the way it worked and it was done in the Vincent de Paul. At our weekly meeting we would get three or four addresses to visit in the course of the following week, of people looking for help. The slips with the addresses were called 'tickets'. There was a particular district that we covered and we got the names and addresses of the people looking for help in our district. We would visit the families or the individuals then. When we would go back to the next meeting we would have to report upon the three, or four, or whatever number of tickets that we had been given.

There was terrible poverty in our area and we got the names of a lot of the very, very poor families. While we were very close to the Coombe, we were visiting around and off Wexford Street, Whitefriar Street, Kevin Street. There were some very poor people around and there were a lot of tenements. We would call and knock on the door and announce ourselves. Someone would say, "It's the Vincent de Paul brothers". We were called a 'brother' in the Vincent de Paul.

Large families lived in one room. They were tenements alright, very much tenements. Conditions people had to live in were dreadful, conditions were absolutely miserable for the people; they were dark, damp and miserable. There might be three or four children on the cold floor, some others down the street, others on the stairs. The stairs my God, you would have to be very careful going up the stairs 'cause the steps of the stairs were....

---

[48] Current value is 23 cent.
[49] Myra House in Francis Street was the premises of the Legion of Mary. It was also used by the St. Vincent de Paul Society.

Well, there would be a bit of an ould board holding two steps together. It was absolutely miserable. When I think about it today when people can report or call out the Corporation because of a slight leak.

We gave out vouchers or 'tickets' for the value of three shillings and sixpence or five shillings.[50] The voucher was given into the local shop or Pierce Redmond's, I can't remember all the shops that would be taking our vouchers. Anyway, there were a number of shops that were accepting St Vincent de Paul vouchers. If the person was a really poor person with a lot of children she got a voucher for five shillings because of the circumstances of her case, but the normal run of the mill was you gave a ticket for three and sixpence which was handed in over the counter for three and sixpence worth of food.

I remember one family with a radio. We took a note of that. There was a radio in the corner. At the Conference meeting you would report on what you found. There would be ten or twelve brothers at the Conference. You'd report that there was a family with a radio, even though it might not be working, but it was there. It was a sign of luxury.

If a person could afford to have a radio she couldn't be considered to be that badly off. The Vincent de Paul had so many poor people to help and you'd imagine that the woman with a radio would understand that too. She could go to a pawnshop and get some money for the radio.

The Conference would decide on what help, if any, people would get. The Conference meeting was like any meeting today, fellas would want to talk and give their opinion. But a lot would depend on what we said and what we thought about the case.

Mr Cowley, as the President of the Conference, asked me what I thought. Well, for me the family had a radio, but it wasn't working for want of a battery. The family seemed to be decent, genuine people. They weren't accustomed to asking the Vincent de Paul for anything. But there came a time when they needed to. I put myself in their position. If I brought the radio to the pawn office, I'd get something for it and then the next week and the next week and the next week I wouldn't have the radio or the chance to get it back. I thought surely to God, if we were to help out that lady this once and get the radio working we could leave the family with the radio. It was company they had in the house and we would be finished with her, and she would be one person who would be very happy as a result of her getting her voucher.

---

[50] Five shillings is 32 cent.

I made my case. The President then said, "I agree with Brother Lynam. If we were to help that woman she'd be one woman to recognise the Vincent de Paul Society for what they are, a Society that wouldn't see you stuck or in poverty, if they could help it".

So the woman was given a few shillings.

There is one case that stands out in my memory. We visited a lady I remember she was sitting by the fire in the room and the grate was empty. "Oh I try to light the fire sometimes at night. I've five of them" she told me. She had the rosary beads in one hand and would pass them to the other. Her story impressed me. I didn't think she was putting on an act. I went to the meeting. I thought I had a good story to tell and I'd lay it on thick. "She said she'd only this, she'd only that, she had nothing coming in. She had lots of children and they all seemed very small".

When I had finished my story they said to me. "That person is a long, long time on our books and it's the same story everytime. But the next time you go back, ask the women "Does the young fella still sell the Herald[51] outside Jacob's[52] or does such and such sell something else and something else" - they were listing off her children - "And the other young fella, ask her is he still working down at the North Wall with the pony and cart. Ask her about all her children next time you go down, and her circumstances, and then come back and tell us what you think." Well, honest to God, I felt awful let down.

Carol Singing

Carol singing was for me recreation. Whatever money was raised in carol singing was for the poor people and there was no problem in sorting that out. But we knew the score about what carol singing was worth to us. We would go carol singing to a place like McCaffrey's Estate, a place outside the Union[53] hospital in James Street. There were a lot of houses there. We had a lot of singers in our Conference, but we were the ones, the fellas, that

---

[51] The Herald was one of the two daily evening papers in Dublin at the time and the only one surviving since the closure of the Irish Press.

[52] Biscuit factory located in Bride Street off Kevin Street before it moved to Tallaght. The old building was later destroyed by fire and the site now houses The Dublin Institute of Technology.

[53] Now St James Hospital. Dublin people for a long time found it difficult to shake off the old name and its Union/pauper/workhouse associations. Originally the House of Industry that established in 1703 both a workhouse for male 'vagabonds' and 'sturdy beggars' and 'idle' and 'disorderly' women found able or fit for labour, and the Dublin Foundling Hospital 'to prevent the exposure, death and actual murder of illegitimate children' and 'to educate and rear children (in care) in the Reformed or Protestant Faith'. Under the South Dublin Poor Law Union, in 1840, the Workhouse was declared fit for the reception of paupers, and the hospital facilities were later expanded. Rebel forces occupied it in 1916. After independence it was renamed St. Kevin's Hospital. It was not a happy day when you were taken to the Union Hospital.

would have to knock on the doors. Bang bang. Next you'd hear someone inside shouting "It's the carol singers, don't answer it". Or if they did come out they would give you a couple of coppers. We had collection boxes for the money.

When we were finished singing and collecting, we would go back to Myra House and count whatever we had in the boxes. We would have very little. We would get very little, but we were lucky to get anything at all, I suppose.

But anyway, this night Tom McSweeney and myself were with the carol singers from the Conference. We were walking up Francis Street, and up to Cornmarket, to get the tram going in the direction of Inchicore. What they had decided this particular night, was to go up to McCaffrey's Estate, to sing up there and to collect some money. Tom and myself decided to take it easy, we had hatched another plan. I had to tie my shoe and he had to tie his shoe or boot and next thing the tram appeared and they all ran to catch it. Sure with us all tied up in our shoes, we couldn't make the tram and shouted to them to go ahead. The fare was only a penny up to McCaffrey's Estate. Anyway, we turned the other way and turned back into town, which we were planning to do all the time. We headed off to town because we were after sampling town on a previous Sunday and there was loads of money in there, if you could get in and at it.

We collected around the pubs. We'd hide the boxes going in the door. If the barman saw the boxes as we were going in, we wouldn't be allowed into the pub. So we'd keep the boxes down by our side, or keep the hand holding the box in our pocket, and walk inside. When we'd be far enough down the pub, fellas would see us collecting money, but the barman wouldn't see us.

In one pub, someone remarked when they saw our boxes "You're a fairly good distance from your Conference, should you not stick to your area?". We explained that we had got separated from our carol party and wouldn't be able to catch up with them and rather than go back with our boxes empty, we'd like to bring back something, so we wanted to give town a chance. The next fella on the high stool didn't mind putting his hand in his pocket or giving us whatever he could really afford.

Of course when the barman would see you he would wonder who you were collecting money for. "We're the Vincent de Paul" we'd explain.
"Well, you know that you are not allowed collect money in this pub."
"Oh we're sorry because up to this we've been to two or three pubs and it didn't make a difference to them".
"Well, we don't allow it here."

As a result we would leave but we'd be happy enough 'cause we would have already covered half the pub and we'd have got half of what we wanted anyway.

We eventually got back to Francis Street. We knew the others would be back after doing their carol singing at about ten o'clock, and we made sure we would be back at about ten too. The boxes were opened and the money was counted. And sure we had got more in our boxes than the carol singing party had got over two nights. Tom and myself weren't good singers anyway. And sure the whole thing was a bit of craic, whether you were singing or not. Raising money for the poor, that's what it was all about.

Getting about Dublin

For a long while I had no bike at all in Dublin. I had cousins who were nice to me and they used to say "its about time you got yourself a bike and save yourself all this walking". I used to travel a lot on trams, there were no buses then and you'd walk the rest of the way. I remember when I was in Chatham Street, the young lad, the messenger boy, who was riding the carrier bicycle, crashed his bicycle and he broke the small wheel in the front. I must have had some sort of a bike at the time. I asked Mrs. Kelly about the wheel, it had been left out in the yard for a while.
"Well, I'd wish someone would take it away, I'm sick of looking at it. If it's any good to you take it " says she.
So I took it, the carrier wheel, and put it on an ordinary bike and I cycled to Mullingar on it, ninety six miles down and back, and I and had a wonderful time. Eventually I bought a bicycle for seventeen shillings and sixpence in a Sale Yard - a second-hand bicycle.

Keeping in touch with the family

My brothers at home in Marlinstown, Pat and Jim, would 'come up to Dublin' for an occasion, it was a rare enough occasion then. They would surely come up to the All Ireland final and they came to Fairyhouse Races too. The women wouldn't be that interested in the football matches. Mary was at home. Josie was in Dublin. She met Brian in Dublin, he worked in a Jeweller's and Pawnbroker's in Parnell Street. After O'Connell's, she went to work for Pacifico Fusco, Italians, at Doyle's corner. It was a very up-market confectionery, very high class. She worked in the shop selling the confectionery. Later, she went to work for Mr Webster, and of course she finished up with her own shop in Dominic Street in Mullingar. Bill came to Dublin after me. Later, Rose came to Dublin, she was fifteen then. She came up to serve her time in Mrs Kelly's Dairy Shop in Gardiner Street opposite Belvedere College. She stayed then out with Josie in Lindsay Road in Glasnevin, I remember going over there for tea. When Rose was a little older she used to go to the Teachers and other dances and hang around with the rest of us. She worked in Pidgeons with Terry McSweeney, Tom McSweeney's younger sister. And Brigid, Treasa's sister, she worked in Pidgeons too. Sure that's how we all knew each other.

Mary never came to Dublin. She stayed at home in Marlinstown. She gave everything to Marlinstown I wouldn't get to see her till I'd get home on holidays. Teresa being the youngest was the last to come to Dublin. She didn't come till after my mother died. She worked at one stage with Treasa in Pidgeons' branch in Inchicore. The girls all went back home eventually and settled. Do you know how Rose met Eugene? Well, she met him in Josie's place in Dominic Street. He was there icing cakes with Brian McCaffrey who was a friend of his, that's a fact. That's why there were always such fantastic wedding cakes made and iced in Mullingar and Longford.

Mother always wrote as I said, and I wrote home once a week. She would hear about everything and was in touch with all the news. I remember Mother writing a note and asking me to have a look at a certain material for a suit for Jim. She had heard that there was some nice material in Burton's. You could only get ready-made suits in Mullingar, but if Jim came up and got measured, he could have a suit made up for him in Dublin. It was at the time that the long-legged trousers became the fashion, it was the end of 'the flaps', the turn-ups. There used to be signs around '50 s. Tailor', advertising the 'Fifty Shilling Tailor'. That was the price of a suit and the making of it by the tailor.

There were always great hooleys in Lilly and Molly Cunningham's place in Glasnevin, especially at the time of an All Ireland. Everyone and anyone would be there, all the lads would be up from the country and all us in Dublin would be there and more besides. And anyone that had a leg under them would be dancing.

Getting home on holidays - more chances from the Coombe

You had no time to get home except at holiday time. You would get home at Christmas time and summertime and you'd always be hoping to have a bank holiday thrown in. If there was a fair chance of you getting home, you'd get home. They were fair to us in Pidgeons in the Coombe.

I would have spent my summer holidays at home. In summer you got a weeks holiday and if you were lucky you would get a few days more. You'd get two or three days at Easter. At Christmas you got three days. You'd always be hoping to get more. If you had anytime coming to you and it was OK with the boss you mightn't have to come back immediately after Christmas, you might be able to take an extra day. You'd check with the other lads first. If you were into a big job, you'd have to come back after the three days, but if you weren't so busy you'd have the chance of an extra day.

We usen't finish up at Christmas until Christmas Eve, and not before seven o'clock in the evening. You wouldn't get to start out for home then, there would be no way of getting home at that time. But on Christmas morning you would walk down to McBerney's on Aston Quay and you'd wait and you'd wait for the Mullingar bus. All the country buses left from Aston Quay, that was before Bus Áras was built. There would be loads of people waiting and travelling with suitcases, boxes, parcels, the lot. The suitcases and parcels would all be put on the roof of the bus and tied down. On the way back to Dublin after the holiday, you'd stop the bus at the end of the road into Marlinstown, at the end of our road where it meets the Dublin Road. You might be lucky, maybe a lad who knew you would spot you and pick you up in a motorcar and give you a lift back to Dublin and you got back that way. I remember there was one night after Christmas, I was coming back to Dublin to the job. It was a really bad night, black and spilling rain. Mother was so anxious to get Pat to leave me out to the bus. Well, the first bus came and passed us by. The second bus came and Pat jumped out into the middle of the road in all the puddles and nearly got killed trying to make sure the bus stopped for me.

During the war years it was difficult enough to get home, there would be no trains or buses at times. In the summer time, as I said, you might cycle home. You could do it in the summer time, you wouldn't do it in winter though. We'd always consider the journey from Dublin to Mullingar to be forty-eight miles. In the summer there was always plenty of activity. There was the work at home and I would be around with the lads. And I would go visiting friends, cousins and relations too. It was great to get home.

I remember once being down with Josie. Jim lent me his new bike and Josie and I went off visiting. On the way back to Marlinstown I remember we were going a bit fast coming round a corner and down a bit of a hill when I skidded in a lump of gravel. Well, I cut my elbow and took the grip off the handlebar with the fall. I had to go to the doctor in town. He made me go off and buy an anti-tetanus dose and he said he'd administer it. Well, the next day we went off to Killucan. I had really been looking forward to visiting everyone, but I had such a pain in my right arm, in the first house we visited I couldn't even lift the teacup to my mouth. I had to ask Josie to make a pact and say that we had had tea in the last house. I just couldn't manage to lift the cup. Could you ever imagine me turning down tea, but that's a fact.

When I was on holidays I'd go down to Ballinreddra too and I used to hang around with the Murray's, Maggie and Annie and Christy Murray.

The war

I wasn't worried during the war. You would hear the odd noise of the planes at night and people would talk about it, about the bombs that dropped or the bombs that dropped three nights previously. There were special nights with Lord Haw Haw[54] and people would talk about what he said and what he didn't say. He used to always start his broadcasts with "Germany calling, Germany calling". He had an accent and it sounded like "Garmany calling, Garmany calling". He used to be broadcasting from Berlin and people were terrified because he used to tell people on the radio where exactly the Town Hall clocks had stopped. The bombs weren't dropping in Dublin, the planes would be flying overhead and flying on and dropping bombs, in Belfast maybe, or wherever. But you would hear the planes coming. You would keep indoors and keep in the dark. We didn't have lights on after dark. You certainly wouldn't be flashing them or anything like that.

At the end of 1940 though, there were a number of bombs that dropped in different parts of the country. There was one in Wexford; we didn't really hear much of the details of that. Then near to Christmas people in Dun Laoighaire saw bombs go off just off the coast and there was damage done in Meath in the New Year. I think the Germans were trying to get Ireland into the war, maybe it was England that was pushing Ireland to get into the war, you wouldn't know what was going on. We were neutral and they didn't like that. When the war was declared De Valera said that Ireland would remain neutral. There were two bombs in Terenure and two people were killed. Then about 20 people were injured when incendiary bombs went off up on the South Circular Road.

The women were scared stiff going around. It was an anxious time. Often you would hear big noises overhead at night from the planes. A lot of the time what you were hearing were AK AK guns. There were British planes with AK AK guns, big powered shells or guns - they would be scaring off the German planes that were carrying the bombs. There was plenty of activity; the AK AK guns fired huge big volleys.

---

[54] William Joyce was nicknamed Lord Haw Haw by a Daily Express journalist because of his aristocratic nasal drawl. In fact he broke his nose in a fistfight in a convent school in Mayo as a child. His was a fascist and was editor and speaker for the German transmitters for Europe. Although it was illegal to listen to his broadcasts, in his hay day he nearly had as many listeners as the BBC. He caused alarm and panic with his tales of a Fifth Column in Britain, his talks about how to treat bombing wounds and his accurate description of the Town Hall clocks that had stopped. The use of the airwaves to get into British (and Irish) homes was a significant innovation in psychological warfare. Joyce was born of an Irish father and English mother in New York in 1906.

You would hear news during the day, and people would talk about what happened the night before. The people would be so long waiting in the shop and we would be so busy, we would only get the outskirts of their stories.

I was staying with my cousin Rose Casserley, in Cabra, in 52 Leix Road, Cabra. I had moved into digs with her after I left Mrs Behan in Church Street. Mrs Casserley, Rose Cunningham, was married to Joe Casserley from Killucan; he was a tram driver. They had three small children, well, they were small enough, they were four, five and seven, all less that ten years of age. Mrs Casserley would be trying to get them to bed. And then she'd be going up and down the stairs to see if they were asleep, she would be frightening them with her worrying. I remember one night this happened. I think the eldest fellow, Paul, was sleeping in my room. Mrs Casserley was walking around the room, praying and talking to herself. "Isn't it terrible? Oh my God what will happen? Oh dear God!

Says I to her "Will you look Mrs Casserley, go up to bed and stop frightening the children, go up to bed. Sure they're not dropping bombs at all, it's just old guns above in the Park to frighten or to be scaring the people away. It's only the old AK AK guns that you are hearing, sure don't mind them".
"Oh thanks be to God" says she, "I am so frightened, I thought it was them bombs again"
"Not at all" says I.

So the next morning we all got up. We were fairly near the church. As I was going over to mass I noticed that there were about five or six people standing on a corner, and four or five at another corner. Someone said "Oh they are talking about the bombs they dropped last night."

When I came from mass I met Mrs Casserley "You're terrible, you're terrible" she said "you made me go to bed last night when all those bombs were dropping above in the Park and the North Strand. Everyone knew about them but I didn't know."

The only thing that was bothering Mrs Casserley was that everyone else was telling her the big news that she missed when she was fast asleep. The result was I got a lot of scolding over that because I was the one that told her to go to bed and not be frightening the children.

But it was very serious and very frightening and people were terrified after the night of the big Dublin bombs.[55] Over at the North Strand by the Five Lamps, a huge bomb was dropped and it killed thirty-eight local people. There were over a hundred people injured. Other bombs fell around Summerhill and the North Circular Road. There were about three hundred houses destroyed or damaged that night too. The bombs that were dropped in the Phoenix Park the same night, damaged part of the Zoo, and blew in the windows of Áras an Uachtaráin and the American Embassy.

People were really scared. It was over the bank holiday weekend, and back in the Coombe, after the weekend, people in the shop they were all talk.

You could go up to the Phoenix Park and see the big crater above the hurling grounds, there beyond the zoo. I don't know what they did with it after - made a pond out of it, the dog pond. On the North Circular Road you could see the houses that had been flattened. The North Strand was devastated, there were huge fires, it was a real blitz.

Things seemed to quieten down after that, at least there were no more big bombs.

Talking about the Casserleys reminds me of another story. Paddy Cunningham, Rose's brother, used to come up from Derryconnor visiting. One time he said he'd bring young Paul back home with him on holiday. Rose was really worried, she was crying that he might kill himself 'cause he'd walk into something. Paul had loads of energy. Anyway when Paul got down to Ballivor, they asked him what he wanted to do. He went out into the yard and he just stood there for ages, they had to go out and get him. The poor child, he had so much space all around him and so many fields that he could run around in, he just stood there, stunned, and didn't know what to do.

---

[55] The night of the Dublin bombs was 30/31 May 1941. Just after 12.00pm, there were signs of explosions at sea and crews abandoning their bomb loads. At 1.30 am the first bombs fell, two 25lb bombs (25 pounds weight), on North Richmond Street and Ruthland Place in the North Inner City. A 250lb bomb was dropped in the Phoenix Park near the dog pond pumping station. At 2.05am, a 500lb German 'land mine' bomb struck the North Strand near the Five Lamps. Later the German government sent apologies and much later sent some compensation for the damage caused.

Meeting the Darling Girl from Clare

The first time I met Miss O'D, I never thought, I'd no notion that she'd ever be Mrs Lynam. Yes, I was as anxious about myself as I was about Miss O'D, this girl I met for the first time on a Monday morning at nine o'clock. This girl was all dressed up in a snow-white, sparkling white shop coat with a dark coat over it, and she on a bicycle. She just flew into the hallway and next thing she was out talking to the boss. The boss said "We have a change of plan Miss O'D", I think he called her Miss O'D or maybe Miss O'Donoghue, but we all knew her as Miss O'D. He was directing her so as she could find her way to Cabra. These directions were all new to me "Up Meath Street, up Church Street, up Grangegorman past the Mental Hospital, then out on to the Cabra Road", these were the directions to where the new shop was to be opened. And there's where she rested.

She was over there and working like the devil, as she always did, and dealing with the customers. Of course she struck me when I first saw her. She was a very smart, good looking, black-haired girl.

The first contact that I would have had with Miss O'D after she went to Cabra was ringing up on the phone, checking on prices in Cabra or something or other. But it's funny to relate that the man that was in charge in Cabra at that time, was a Mr. Lynam. There was a Mr. Lynam and a Mr. Lynam, but Mr Lynam in Cabra was a different man altogether. He was no relation and a much older man than me, at that time.

From the point of view of business, I would have been in contact with Treasa and that. I was well, I suppose, I was keenly interested. I wasn't falling over her, or anything like that. As a matter of fact I introduced other fellas to her. Fellas would come in to me, "Any chance that you would put in a word for me with Miss O'D?"
"Will you go leave me alone for goodness sake...Oh alright, OK...Well, I'll tell her you were asking after her."
That's the way it used to be. I remember one chap, he was in the Vincent de Paul Society, he was much older than Treasa was at the time, and he was thrilled. I think they went out on a couple of occasions, but that was all. There were always a lot of fellas interested. She had no problem getting fellas. She was sparkling at any time.

I do remember the first time we went out. The Legion was running a function in the Four Courts Hotel. Our Presidium was invited to it. I went along to it, along with a couple more.

A ladies Presidium, I think, organised the function with a gent's Presidium so that we would have a night's dancing together, I'm not sure. Anyway I danced with Treasa and then asked Treasa how was she getting home.

"I'm walking," says she.

We left together. "I'm going up this way," she said as we came out of the hotel, which meant we were heading in the Phoenix Park direction. The next turn then led off to the Cabra Road. It was the self-same way, if you can follow me, that she took to Cabra that first morning that I saw her in the Coombe. I remember clearly the directions she was given, that first time I saw her, when Tom Cowley directed her, from the Coombe to Cabra Road, up by Grangegorman. So I walked with her that way and chatted her on the way up. I asked her what she was doing on such and such a night.

"Maybe we could go to the pictures together?".

She said yes, and from there on we began to see each other.

She was living in digs over the shop in the Cabra Road with Seamus and Flor Lynam and their two daughters Imelda and Marie, and that's where she lived for quite a while. They owned the premises and Mr Lynam was managing the shop for Pidgeons. I discovered too, that first night, that she was in the Legion of Mary, I don't know when Treasa joined the Legion. She joined the Legion, I think it was in Barry's Hotel, everyone in the country knows Barry's Hotel, off Mountjoy Square in Denmark Street. I think the Legion over that area asked to have their meetings over there.

So she was in the Legion of Mary and I was in the Legion. As a result there were a lot of functions. One section of the Legion would be giving another section support, selling tickets for functions to each other's Presidium and helping each other out. The Legion was a very big organisation at that time. Treasa was Vice President of her Presidia. She had a big post in the Legion. There would have been about twenty or thirty people in her Presidia. Treasa's Legion activity was on a Sunday morning at eight o'clock getting kids up and out of bed and dressed and then bringing them to mass in Marlborough Street. That would have been her Legion work for the week. The Legion had 'Aches' like meetings, with talks, lectures and prayers. And of course there were all sorts of social outings. Treasa wasn't in the Vincent de Paul. Women were not allowed to be members of the Vincent de Paul then. I don't know if it has changed. Although it had a religious aspect, it gave out help, and food and alms to the poor; it was not a prayerful organisation.

And there were always hooleys. As I said the Cunninghams had great hooleys. I was often at a hooley till six o'clock in the morning, with bagpipes and loads of music. And sure we would be drinking tea and milk. Sure most of us were pioneers.[56] You'd leave the hooley at six in the morning and you'd always get mass at half six on a Sunday morning on the way home. You'd get home, sleep till dinnertime and then be down to Croke Park for a match at one thirty.

We would go to the pictures too, you could go down to 'the Phibo' to the pictures. I remember going to the pictures to the Carlton for nine pence[57] in the afternoon, or you could go upstairs in the Savoy. One time I noticed that "How Green Was My Valley" was on in the Savoy with some great Irish actors so I decided to treat myself. Well, there wasn't a green spot in sight – it was all black, not a bit of green in it, it was all about the coalmines and there wasn't a green spot in sight. The one film that I remember is 'The Life of a Bengal Lancer' in the Capital; I don't know why I remember that. Treasa liked 'Gone with the Wind', that was a dear film, but naturally being the gentleman I paid. I remember after taking her on a Monday night. I asked her after if she liked the film. She did. I discovered afterwards that she had seen the film three times, but it was her first time seeing it with me. But fellas couldn't be affording to take girls out to the pictures too often. You'd more often go to the ceili and old-time.

Telling yarns

Then there'd be nights that you might end up playing cards or telling yarns in someone's digs. There were so many yarns and stories. There was one story I remember hearing about fellas who lived at the back of a pub up in Harold's Cross. The fella who lived in the upstairs flat, would sometimes come in late at night with a few jars on him and he'd wake the others up with the noise he'd make. Their flat was at the end of the stairs. So they decided to get their own back. One night they got an old heavy boot, put a nail through the toe, and nailed it onto the bottom step of the stairs. They got a string and looped it through the loop at the back of the boot, and then hung the string over the door of their flat at the bottom of the stairs. Well, your man arrived in, in the early hours of the morning. They heard him closing the door and starting up the stairs. There was no light of course. When he was on about the third step they pulled the string and lifted up the heel of the boot, and let it drop on the step, clop, they pulled the string again and let the heel drop, clop, and again they pulled the string and let it drop, clop. The poor fella could hear footsteps following him up the stairs but he couldn't see a living thing. He went up a few more steps

---

[56] A 'Pioneer' was a member of the Pioneer Total Abstinence Association, a Temperance Movement founded in 1898 by Fr. James Cullen and four women in St Francis Xavier Church in Gardiner St. In the early days it was confined to women. At Confirmation, young people are offered the option of 'Taking the Pledge' and abstaining from all alcoholic drink till they are 18 years old.
[57] Nine pence is approx. 5 cent.

and the footsteps kept following him. Well, he scurried up the stairs and the lads kept pulling the string and lifting and dropping the heel, deliberately and slowly, clop...clop...clop.... Well, they scared the living daylights out of him. I'd say the fella wasn't worth tuppence. Nobody ever said a word and they did it on him another night. They never saw the poor fella in the upstairs flat again. Lord God almighty, isn't it shocking the things fellas got up to.

I remember there was another story, about a fella who went visiting neighbours in the country. It was a dark and dreary night and the lads had met up to play cards. But sure one thing borrowed another and they began to tell stories, I suppose what you might call haunted stories. Well, there were all sorts of stories told, and a whole pile of stories about 'happenings' in the area going back a good few years. Anyway this one fellow had to leave earlier than the others. He wasn't too happy to be going out into the night on his own, after the night of stories, but off he went home anyway, across the fields. Well, no sooner had he gone than the rest decided to play a trick on him. They tied a lamp on the dog and after a while they sent the dog out after him. Well, talk about running for your life. The poor fella didn't know what was coming after him, all he could see was this light close to the ground, moving and shaking, and coming after him through the grass.

There was another story about a fella who was convinced his flat was haunted. He'd be in bed at night and suddenly the room would light up, a flash of yellow light would come into the room and pass over his bed. It happened every night just after midnight; he was petrified in the bed. He couldn't figure it out and he was convinced he was being haunted. Sure what was happening was someone in a house a distance away, was coming in off a late shift. When they opened their door, the light from the hall reflected off a mirror inside on a wall and bounced the light at an angle into your man's flat. Poor fella he didn't wait around for the explanation.

Mick Murphy, Tom and Lillian Byrne, July 1940. Mick and Lillian were the stalwarts of Pidgeon's when I joined. Great, great, people and great friends to me.

Treasa O' Donoghue. My lovely rose of Clare.

Outside 29 The Coombe. We were offering farm butter then at a shilling a pound.

(L-R) Butch Kavanagh, Tom Mc Sweeney, Tom
and Kevin Maguire at Fairyhouse Races.

(L-R) Tom Mc Sweeney, George Mc Caffrey, Ned Lenihan,
Brian Mc Caffrey and Tom in the Phoenix Park.

N.B.—The Purveyor is requested to enter on the back the particulars, quantities and prices of the provisions supplied

✠

SOCIETY OF ST. VINCENT DE PAUL.

Our Lady of Victories.

Conference of...

day of..............................193...

Give Provisions to the value of.................shillings and.................pence

to .... *Mrs. B........*

29 New Bride Street

To Mr.......... *Redmond*

Purveyor

.... *Wexford*..........Street

P. Cowley

PRESIDENT.

*Please write the number of shillings and pence IN WORDS, not in figures.

P.P.D.—100M.

St. Vincent de Paul Docket.

Treasa outside the Pro Cathedral with children from the Marlborough Street area.

Dear Tom

Would you please call to Burtons & see how Jim would fair out if he went up before May is out, We hear now you cannot get anything only utility suits in the city wth without turn up on the trousas. & without pockets is this so

we want him to get a sports rig out & he is anxious to get a suit himself so please call & see what things are like before he goes up he is talking of a grey we heard there was three nice pieces in a shop in town yesterday but what about the tailor

Your mother

A letter from my mother.

Michael Dunning and Tom outside Pidgeon's, August 1942.

Bill and Tom in the 'wooden gate' field,1941.

Teresa, Bill, Rita Cox and Jim,1941.

Jim, Josie, Brian McCaffrey, Maureen Murray, Gerard Cox & Mary.

A pleasure trip up the Inney River near Ballinalack. 1941.
Maggie Murray, Tom, Rita Cox and Maureen Murray.

(L-R) Teresa, Mother, Annie Murray, Mrs Tom Cox of Dublin, Rita Cox, Tom and Rose.

Life during the Emergency

The time was known as 'The Emergency' because De Valera declared a state of emergency when the war broke out. Then Churchill put restrictions on the export of British goods to Ireland. I suppose he couldn't have been happy when Dev announced that we would remain neutral, that we wouldn't take part in the war and we wouldn't take sides. De Valera then encouraged the country to produce our own foodstuffs. We couldn't produce tea, and people got really desperate for tea, but there was a big campaign to grow wheat. Land that had hardly been tilled before, was now producing wheat, the quality naturally wasn't as good as the best of imported wheat. When the home milled flour was baked it produced a dark coloured loaf, and the texture was rough. People would be going mad for 'white' bleached flour.

The other big change was the number of Dublin people going to the bog. Turf cutting was a big thing, Dubliners would be up the Dublin mountains at the weekends, cutting turf, stacking it, drying it and taking it home. There was no British coal.

Later on during the Emergency gas and electricity supplies were drastically cut. Gas was rationed, even after the war. There was only full pressure at certain times; at off peak times the pressure was really low, I suppose they couldn't turn off the gas completely for fear of air locks in the pipes. People would be trying to get a bit of gas without being caught by the glimmerman. He used to come round checking up on people, he'd check if you had been using gas by putting his hand on the gas ring, if it was warm then you could have your supply cut off.

Do you know that song from that time?

> *"Bless'em all, bless 'em all, bless 'em all,*
> *The long and the short and the tall*
> *Bless De Valera*
> *And Sean McEntee*
> *To hell with their dark bread*
> *And half ounce of tea[58]*
> *For we're sayin'*
> *Goodbye to them all"*

And the song goes on.

---

[58] A half-ounce is 14.17 grams. Your ration of tea was 14.17 grams per week. This was particularly difficult for families who would normally use a kilo of tea per week.

Ration Books

Tea, sugar, butter, flour, petrol were all rationed, bread and flour were rationed too at different times. Only doctors could get petrol at one stage. At one time you would hardly see a motor car around.

The post office delivered a ration book to every household every week. Everyone was registered at the post office. It was like the way you would get a book of stamps at the post office now at Christmas time, but they were bigger ones than that. You got a ration book as a right. The book was full of coupons. When you went shopping you handed in your ration coupon at the counter and paid as normal.

There were different letters, one for sugar, one for soap - different letters or numbers for the different rationed goods. Some people used to cut the coupon with the letter 'L'; they would cut it at the corner of the 'L' and try that way to make out that they had two coupons with the letter 'I'. What people would give for coupons. They were always trying to swap them.

Sometimes people would hand over coupons or they would slip in, say, one for soap, and try and get tea.
You would say "That one is for soap Mrs"
"Did I give you the one for tea son?"
"No Mrs"
"God I must have lost it"

Tea was always bothering people, they never had enough tea. Everything was rationed, but you would usually manage the coupons in your book, but never the tea. The tea always ran out first. You got a ration of a half-ounce of tea a week.

There was a big black market too. "Any chance of a bit of tea?" was all you ever heard at the time. Tea was like gold dust. People would give anything for it. There would be people offering tea on the black market. After people bought it they would discover that the whole bottom half of the bag was only sawdust. People who bought a chest of tea on the black market probably thought they were getting away with it until they discovered that at least four inches at the bottom of the chest was sawdust. There were all sorts of scams and fiddles going on.

Pidgeons was responsible for rationing the tea that we gave out. Our allowance would come from Brook Bond in London. It would come in a chest. We would have a certain amount of tea to get us over a period. Every ounce of it, every half-ounce of it, had to be accounted for. We had to file every single one of the coupons and count all our coupons.

We had problems with the tea in Sundrive Road. I was managing the Coombe and Mrs Cowley, the boss's wife, was managing the shop in Sundrive Road. She was a very nice person to very nice people, if she made them out to be very nice people. Of course, people were always being very nice to her because they might get a little extra tea and that would make all the difference. She was a bit soft like that. It came to the point that too much tea was missing and they just weren't able to find it or account for it. It wasn't stolen - that wouldn't enter into it. Evidently this situation had to stop, as Pidgeons were responsible for accounting for all of the tea that we got.

Mr Cowley decided that I was the one to sort the problem of the missing tea and I was given the job by Mr Cowley. Up in Sundrive Road, I turned over the ration books, and turned over the ration books, over, and over, and over. Mrs Cowley looked at me.
"How were we going to get this sorted out", I asked her.
"Well, Mr. Lynam" says she, she spoke with a bit of an accent, "That's another job for your fairy wand".

White flour was always in great demand too. People used to sieve the brown coarse wheaten flour, trying to get at what wasn't white flour, but the more ground parts of the wheaten, leaving behind the husks and that. They had no way of grinding the flour, it was pretty coarse. You'd hear plenty of stories. "Oh such and such a mill down the country was giving out ground flour last week" or "Such and such a one got a stone of ground flour". It would be nothing for some people to travel a big distance in search of white flour. They would be all planning, there were so many people planning to go down the country, to get a bit of white flour.

The Pidgeons' head office was in the Coombe and Lillian was in charge of the office. All of the branch managers had to bring their cash and receipts and the coupons to head office. Poor Treasa, they used to have endless trouble in Cabra with tea dockets. It was a real headache. Lillian was well able for it. I always say there is nothing too difficult if you are trained to do it. You just keep within the lines - there are rules for everything.

Foodstuffs and the war

I suppose during the war we got in on the chance to send foodstuffs to England. We used to take a leaf or two out of the telephone book, I shouldn't be telling this, well, someone in England or coming back from England would do it for you. And you would go down the list and pick out what you thought was a factory or a shop or a business. And you would send them a leaflet, like the way people advertise today, telling them what you could offer and giving them an address. You would get an order "Please forward us so many cases of...." Whatever it was they were looking for.

We used to send what we called 'collared head' to England during the war; it was pig's head really. Pigs' cheeks would be boiled, taken out and all the bones would be removed from the head. Then it would be put through a machine. The result would be that it would be coarsely minced and pressed. Brawn would be made in the same way. The skin of the pig's cheeks, ears, all parts except the brains and the bones, would be put into the machine for mixing and pressing as well. A certain amount of gelatine would be put in the mix. The gelatine would be added to keep it firm and bind it all together, so that it was solid. You'd turn it out on a block and put it in a bowl to set. When it would be turned out it would be just like turning out a pudding at Christmas. This was sent to England. We wouldn't be sending it away in bowls, we would take it out and wrap up so many pieces, they were firm enough to wrap. We would put them in a box in the fridge before we sent them away in the morning, and it would be perfect till it got to the other side on the next day. Well, we never got any complaints anyway.

Then there was a time when we had no bowls, we weren't able to get bowls, and we would put the mix in sweet tins, Mackintosh's sweet tins. There was one really popular tin, we would fill that up to the level of whatever it was, I think it was about four pounds weight and it would set in that. We would put so many of these sweet tins in a case and send them off. When the tins got there, all they had to do was to dip the tin into boiling water to thaw out the frost on the outside, and then the collared head would then easily drop out of the tin. Other than that, they could just as easily slice it out of the tin. The tins were perfectly clean.

We used to send out cans of stuff too - tinned fruit, known as 'two-and-a-half's'. It was a large tin, a two and a half pound tin; you don't see them in the shops now. We'd advertise in the paper in England and offer tinned fruit for sale. We would be contacted with an order. People would send the money to us and we would send out whatever they wanted, strawberries, mixed fruits, whatever it was they wanted, or jam, we would send 'two-and-a-half's' of jam too. We would pack and send them off, three tins in a box.

We would buy the tins of fruit in caseloads from the wholesaler. I don't know where they would come from, England maybe, they could have come from anywhere. We used to buy cases of apricots, peaches, pears, strawberries, there were two dozen tins in a case. All we did was transfer the tins and pack them in small boxes of three's. We bought in corrugated cardboard boxes, they would come in to us flat, and we would make up the box and seal it at both ends. We'd put three tins of fruit in a box, apricots, pears, strawberries; you would always give people a variety in the box. Then we'd tie them with string, put a label on them and send them out. As fast as we could get the three tins into the boxes and tie them up, they would go out. We'd take them down to James Street to the Post Office and put the labels on. The person in the post office would sign the docket for you and take them away. They would put them behind the counter and then they would go off in skips or whatever to the main sorting office and then by sea to England. Of course there was lots of money to be made, it wouldn't be done otherwise.

They were going mad for the tinned fruit in England; they couldn't get enough of it. It became a racket. Lord of Mercy on Dick Kavanagh, he use to drive the horses for us in Pidgeons, when we only had horse transport. He'd park the horses at the bottom of the Coombe; he had his stables for the horses down there. His girlfriend used to live on the Northside. She wrote to the paper in England and put in an add offering tins of fruit. They wouldn't know if the address she had given was a house or a shop or whatever. She had the orders and the cheques sent to her house and she would go over to the husband-to-be, they weren't married at the time, and he would pack them in a little room off where the horses were stabled. They were doing a right trade. They got in on the craic too. They had a little business on the side, they just got in on the packing and they were as good as anyone else. It was the very same tinned fruit as we had. He got his boxes from Smurfit too, down at the old Theatre Royal, beside O'Connell Street, that's where the corrugated cardboard boxes came from. Smurfit made a fortune making the boxes that were being sent to England during the war.

During the war I wouldn't say there were many rackets, but I think people were using their wit to make a few bob. You couldn't tin foodstuffs, but you could bottle foodstuffs. People would get tins, open them up, put the contents into bottles and then send them off to England. There was a huge trade in supplying food to Britain and many big fat cheques were received in return. And sure they used to say that England needed to win the war.

Mincemeat Joe

You ask about 'Mincemeat Joe'. Well, he was big business. JF Downes, they were a big manufacturer. Joe Griffin was the man behind the business. He was well known as a man that was well capable of beating the system. He used to make and bottle sauce. He was making and bottling Downes Belmont Sauce. It was something like HP sauce, but it would be nothing like the quality of HP sauce. It was just brown sauce and he had to put flavourings in it and a certain amount of preservatives. But he was sending out sauce that hadn't enough preservatives in it. Well, there was one big batch that was in the Liverpool docks. It got a little delayed there, over a weekend. On Monday they thought bombs were going off, the whole cargo of sauce blew their corks, the yeast caused explosions and blew the corks off the bottles. There was a story going around that two men were employed to do nothing else but sweep up the corks and clean up the mess.

Joe Griffin was always a 'cash on order' man, and he was one man as I said who knew how to beat the system. Then he got into another racket after that, with mincemeat. He got into canning mincemeat and he started sending that out. That started to come back, it wasn't up to the mark and he lost on that one. I don't know if he lost money on that, that was his business, I'm just telling you what he was game for, he was more than game for making money. He was a chancer of the first order and he was making money. He had it all up here, but he lost his head, he went for too much.

One thing that he did make, that I had some involvement in, were the jellies. He had a man from Terenure, who was his agent and he had his office in Thomas Street beside the Library, Thomas Street Transport Agency I think it was called. He would go around taking orders. He would have a sample with him. He explained that they were packing jellies, in two dozen packs. Like the Chivers jelly, you could break off bits. He'd take the order and the cash, and promise that there would be delivery within a week. And he sent out the delivery within the week. The jellies went like hot cakes; people were going mad for the jellies. We thought if they were selling so well, the next time we should get a bigger order, and we did. The result was that people would ask for two packages, and ask could they not buy three packages. They were sold but people didn't use the jellies up immediately. By the end of the third week, a poor woman would discover that there was fur growing on them, they were fermenting. It would start off that the jelly would be half an inch thick and tight in a cardboard box, but after a while you could rattle the jelly inside the box with the amount of fur that was growing on them. Joe Griffin was cute enough, he always demanded and got cash on order. You'd be happy enough if you used the jelly the day you got it, but if it was left for any length of time it would grow and half the box would have turned to fur.

He had the mincemeat factory out in Tallaght. A lorry would go out from the quays with the wooden boxes of dried fruit that he imported, currants and raisins. I'm not sure what he put in to make the mincemeat mix, some currants, but no raisins, some treacle, but he put something in to moisten the fruit. The mixture was put in jars and a cap put on the jar. Griffin was doing a roaring trade with the mincemeat; of course that was until all the stuff started coming back. There was one fella who used to get his wooden boxes and he would turn them into firewood, he made a fortune out of selling kindling[59] from Griffin's empty dried fruit boxes.

He bought a racehorse for a great deal of money. Well, his horse won the Grand National and he won a second Grand National. He invited hundreds to a huge do[60] in the Gresham. He ordered a chicken per head for everyone at this powerful do, and that was in the war years.

He bought a house out in Templeogue and he built a big dancehall out at the back of it, with a maple floor, the lot. He invited the whole Government, Ministers and all, out to the house and gave them a great night out there. He was well in.

One thing he was got for, was a product for improving the growth in grass. He had an agency somewhere down the country. He had someone going round with a sample of the product and showing how it could get results. Ironmongers stocked the stuff and farmers around the country bought it. But then he was discovered mixing large amounts of washing soda with the stuff; they both had the same texture. He was punished for that I think, but sure he was up to a rake of things. He was making handsome money beating the system, but in the end the system caught up with him.

Another swing he had was at Dublin Airport. On the front of the newspaper there was a big photograph of him on the tarmac "Joe Griffin Bringing the First Consignment of French Strawberries to Ireland". He was there photographed with some of the leading people of the day, meeting the plane and receiving his first cargo of French strawberries. He was everywhere.

Well, when the bottom fell out of the bucket and he was caught, he ended up in Mountjoy.[61] I was talking to my old friend Mick Reynolds, Mick who was with me in the

---

[59] Small pieces of wood to light a fire. A bundle of wooden sticks, 10 or 12 sticks were bound with a rubber band or a piece of twine. They were sold everywhere and were very popular as firelighters.
[60] a big formal party, with the best of food and drink and entertainment.
[61] Mountjoy prison in Dublin.

Mayo. He had his own shop later in Meath Street, and poor Mick he had got caught with a lot of the jellies.

"Will you ever forget Griffin? They caught up with him at last," says Mick. "Last year all the Ministers were the guests of Joe Griffin, now Joe Griffin is the guest of the Ministers".

A man I did business with told me he saw Griffin in Mountjoy. He was delivering eggs to the prison and Joe Griffin was one of the prisoners working in the yard unloading the eggs from the delivery van. Prisoners weren't allowed to talk, but he said "There was Joe Griffin, sucking through two fingers, like the way you would suck on a fag",[62] it was his way of trying to ask for a cigarette. What the delivery men would do is drop a cigarette on the ground at the side of the van. You could never give or hand anything to a prisoner.

Dublin Characters

There were a lot of characters around Dublin at the time, they were talked about and they became famous. Bang Bang[63] was probably the most well known. His real name was Thomas Lord Dudley. He went all around the Liberties shooting people with his gun, which was an old black key. Bang bang he'd shout, as he would jump on the bus, to protect the people with his gun. The number fifty bus was his stagecoach. I knew him well when I worked in the Coombe. He'd come in to do business with us; he'd have Vincent de Paul vouchers to get goods from us. He lived in Newmarket, near O'Keeffe's the knackers. Poor Bang Bang would be in a complete sweat from being chased or from chasing the bad fellas.

He was as thin as a whippet, I'd say about eight stone. The kids were always running after him. He would come to the door of Pidgeons and slip inside for a rest.
"Its over. Its over" he'd shout, trying to catch his breath.
He got to the stage where he wasn't able to look after himself and he moved to the Old Folks Home in Cork Street.

Johnny Forty Coats[64] was another character around the Coombe. You would see him begging in and around Francis Street. Poor fella he was another man that the children knew was always good for a chase.

---

[62] a cigarette.

[63] Thomas Lord Dudley born 1906 and died in 1981, he got his name from his constant shouting bang bang, as he went around shooting people with his gun - a vault key. He was abandoned by his parents and raised by the Dominican nuns. He died in the Old Folks Home in Cork Street.

[64] Johnny Forty Coats real name was Jack Russell. Jack lived in a coal shed in the Coombe.

Then there was President Keely. He'd walk up Lord Edward Street wearing a tall silk hat with Keely written on it. 'Vote Number 1 Keely'. In Croke Park you'd hear him moving around "OKey Kee ley" and he doing a bit of an action. He always got a great reception.

When I was in Chatham Street, I knew Faith Hope and Charity. He used to paint a big shamrock just outside the main gates to St. Stephen's Green at the top of Grafton Street and in each of the leaves he would write Faith, Hope and Charity. He had beautiful, beautiful printing in the middle of the shamrock, massive, it was very good.

Damn the Weather was another famous man, of course got his name from his constant cursing "Damn the weather, damn the weather". I didn't come across him myself though. There was another fellow who had a little dog that used to smoke a pipe, and the man himself would have a box of snuff. He used to sit outside Newell's of Grafton Street, a ladies shop just right beside Woolworth's.

Hurling, Camogie, Legion outings, picnics, and plenty of craic on a Sunday

On a Sunday Treasa would be playing a camogie match or I would be playing a hurling match. I'd be up at her match or she'd be at my hurling match. Treasa played for CIE and Colmcilles Club would be supported by the Camogie Club. Or on the afternoon we'd have an outing. A big gang of us would go off on Sundays, the camogie girls and the 'colmers' as we called them. We'd all cycle to the Pine Forest or Bohernabreena for a picnic. We were always going on outings. Wherever it was anyway we'd usually have hurleys and camogie sticks with us, we'd generally be coming from a match in the Park. The sticks would be tied on to the bicycle and the gear in the boot of the bike and we'd head off. We'd fool around a bit, maybe play a bit of ball, whatever we did; sure we enjoyed ourselves anyway.

Keen to capture the moment - Taking photos

I took the photo of Treasa in Glendalough, the one I keep in my wallet. I had about twenty cameras, but I never had a new camera. I bought them in auction rooms and places. They were all fairly good. I'd go home on holidays and I'd take about three or four rolls of films. They would all want photos. They'd say, "Here he comes with the camera." I'd go to the bog with the camera and catch the fellas cutting turf. It was on the bog that I first discovered how to boil water in a paper bag - make a note of that - to boil water in a paper bag. I can give you a demonstration, it can be done.[65]

---

[65] Tom did in fact give a demonstration when he was on holidays in Camus, Conemara at the home of Máire Uí Ghiobúin in 1996.

The day I cut the eye, my version of events

You want to know how I got the four stitches on my eyebrow? I was playing a match up at the fifteen acres in the Phoenix Park. Well, I went in under a ball with another chap. He was pulling against me and I don't know which one of us was at fault but I got a gash over the eye anyway. There was a John's man[66] there and he just bandaged me up and said you better get down to the hospital with that. Dr. Steven's Hospital was always the hospital for the Phoenix Park. If you went down to Steven's Hospital to the accident department there was always a queue of people waiting for their turn to get bandaged up or whatever, because there were always accidents coming from the Park. So I decided anyway, I'd cycle down to the Mater,[67] I had the bike with me at the fifteen acres.

On this occasion we had togged out in one of the dressing rooms in one particular clubhouse. I made my way over to the dressing room and I just pulled up my pants over my football togs and put on my jacket. Whatever else I was carrying I just put it in the boot of the bicycle and set off for the Mater hospital, down the North Circular Road as it is today. They had called for an ambulance for me, but as I was cycling out Parkgate Street I met the ambulance going in. I had a cap pulled over the head and the eye to keep the bandage in place. Of course when they went up to the fifteen acres they were looking for me. But Billy Phelan was there and he'd been a bit injured so they took him in the ambulance instead. I arrived into the Mater anyway, and I heard, "Ah another one." I remember well the nurse cleaning off my head and face and my eye. I got four stitches and the nurse bandaged me up. As the nurse was dressing it she said to the other nurse "Now you know why I told Dick Stokes to give up this hurling lark".

I went up to Mrs Casserley for my dinner; I was staying with her at that time. I remember Mrs Casserley saying "My God Almighty Save Us", when she saw the bandage across my head. "I knew that would happen someday". But I felt great. After the dinner I told her I was off again.
"No not again" says she.
"No its alright" says I, "I'm going down to Croke Park".

I remember going into Croke Park with the bandage over my forehead and over my eye, and I saw one, if not two matches that afternoon.

---

[66] St John's Ambulance provided first aid and emergency cover at public events.
[67] The Mater Hospital on the northside of Dublin city centre.

There was one thing about hurling, if you were cut and you were bleeding, you'd be taken off. If you stopped bleeding, you could go back on. At that time, if someone got a bang of a hurley stick people would say "Oh my God, he got split open". If you cut your finger, sure you would loose a fair amount of blood before you would get it bandaged. Well, of course if you got a cut on your forehead over the eye, you would have a fair amount of blood all around your face. I'm sure it looked really awful, especially with someone drying it off with a bit of a sponge or whatever they might have, out of the kit bag.

In the evenings I used to get it dressed in the old St Vincent's Hospital when it was there on Stephen's Green. It healed in a couple of weeks. But having the bandage and all that was never half as bad as when it was getting better. The more it got better, the blacker it got. I was working in the Coombe at the time. A week after getting cut it was worse 'cause the people would be laughing at me or giving out to me or that. It went black and purple and yellow. I was a sight.

Outings and Dances

We spent a lot of our time in Barry's Hotel at that time, with the Camogie Club supplying the girls and the hurling club supplying the fellas. Our clubs, well, they were arm and arm with each other, one supported the other and vice versa. We used to have smashing dances in Barry's Hotel. The Knocknagow Social, well, the world and his mother knew about it. It was the place to be. It was on every Monday night and we would be down early. The first dance would be early, about half eight or nine o'clock. We'd sum it up; it was like looking at the flowers over there. We would be looking for, and waiting for, the set dance.

Tom McSweeney was the MC, the Master of Ceremonies. We'd ask him to give us the nod in plenty of time before he called the set dance, so that when he called the next dance as a set dance, we would already be all organised. We knew very well that over there, were three or four girls, the best dancers in the place. They would be all sitting out. Before McSweeney ever called the dance, we would have had our dancers all picked out, and we were ready to move quickly. We'd be over to them and get them up on the floor. The other lads would be still looking around but we would already be up in the corner, right up beside the band with our four couples for our set, and the best dancers. Well, other lads' timing was never as good as ours, it wasn't anything as good as ours, and they were never as organised. And there would be other people still struggling to get out on the floor and you'd hear McSweeney call for another two couples to try to make up a full set on some other part of the dance floor.

There was the Timmy Whelan Ceili Band, a fantastic band. He was a beautiful, a beautiful, beautiful musician and he used to step dance as well. Every turn of our dance would be as tight and we would finish every figure to the music.

We'd dance the sets, I think it was the Caledonian and apart from the sets we would have the ceili dances - the Siege of Ennis and the Walls of Limerick and a great selection of old-time waltzes. Generally all the camogie players that we would know would be at the Knocknagow.

On Tuesday night there would be another great ceili on. It was the Leeside Social in Barry's. There would be great dancers at that too. There would be dances on every night, but they wouldn't be our dances. Different Clubs in Dublin would have their dances in Barry's Hotel on different nights.

So it was a fair old bit of craic and then every Sunday there would be the Legion of Mary functions, outings and various things. Treasa and I, we saw each other and met for ages, till we nearly got tired looking at each other (laughter).

Bank Holiday at Fairyhouse Races. Take your pick.

Fairyhouse Races. (L-R) Mickey Murtagh, Pat, Paddy Lesley,
Bill, Joan Cosgrave, Maire, Treasa, Mary Teresa.

Pine Forest 1942.

Bohernabreena May 1942.

Columcille lads in the Pheonix Park 1942.

Treasa and some of her camogie pals.

Teresa, Tom, Mary, Treasa, in Marlinstown.

1942.

Ben and Brigid.

(L-R) Teresa, Treasa, Pat, Mary, Maureen Murray, Jim, Elsie.

Another day at the races. (L-R) Maire's friend,
Brigid, Tom, Treasa, Maire.

M. Cox, Treasa, Billy Hutchin, Rose, Brigid, Sheila,
in the Phoenix Park 1943.

(L-R) Brian, Josie, a friend, Brigid, Ben, Pat and Jim in the blanket.

Tom and greyhounds outside the 'Cup and Saucer', Marlinstown.

Treasa at Baltrasna Bridge.

Treasa and Tom McSweeney battering it out at the Knocknagow Social in Barry's Hotel in 1943.

Treasa a champion camogie player.

Treasa, the star camogie player

Treasa played for club and County. She played fullback on the Dublin team. She wasn't great, she was brilliant. I only ever played junior hurling with Colmcilles, I wasn't good enough to play senior, but Treasa was one of the best in the CIE club and as I said, a great Dublin player. We used all follow the matches; Colmcilles were great followers of the camogie club and vice versa. Treasa played a lot of matches in Parnell Park, which has now been developed as the Dublin County grounds near Whitehall.

There would be friendly matches outside Dublin and we'd organise our own transport or hire a bus and we'd all go to the inter-county matches too. It would just be a case of "Where are the lads going?", that could be the camogie players or the hurlers, and then we would be all off, and sure we'd sing the whole way home. Whoever would be around would go, Rose would be there, Máire, Sheila, Brigid and Ben. Ben would be a good follower; he wasn't all that interested in football or hurling. Later Brigid and Ben used to go off and do the things they were interested in. Of course we were all up in Belfast for the All Ireland Camogie Final when Dublin played Antrim and Treasa played a great game. Dublin lost by a disputed goal, which Treasa always believed should not have been allowed. But being the great sportswoman that she was, she accepted defeat... well, the way somebody else put it was 'graciously'.

Ben McDonald refereeing in Ballinasloe

There was one particular, now famous, camogie match in Ballinasloe. I was the iompair[68] at that match, Ben was the referee. Dublin were playing Galway in Ballinasloe on home ground. The official referee didn't show up and they were going around crazy looking for a referee. The man running the Dublin team wouldn't let anyone from Galway referee the match, they could be showing a slight bit of favouritism towards the Galway girls. So they decided to get a neutral person, and they got Ben McDonald. He was from Wicklow and he was supposed to be neutral.

Well, Ben did it. I think he was trying to oblige the girls. He didn't know how serious it was, and he wouldn't have been following camogie as much as I would be, he wasn't as clued in. I was asked to do 'ref' but I couldn't, I was too close. Sure how could I referee? Anyway they agreed that I was a bit close and I got off the hook. I said I didn't mind doing iompair, but not referee.

---

[68] Iompair is the Irish word for umpire. In a Gaelic football, camogie, or hurling game the linesman is the iompair.

At that time we had all the great Dublin camogie players including Treasa. We knew them, and Ben knew them but the officials didn't know that he knew them. Sure he was a Wicklow man. But sure he was going out with Treasa's sister Brigid and he knew them all well, from outings and picnics.

Anyway the game started and there was a score, and Galway were winning, and soon winning fairly well. Then Dublin were catching up. The next thing Dublin started to lead and then Galway took the lead again and someone said, "It's not looking that good for this Dublin team". Galway had some very good players on their team as well, but they were very hard camogie players, very tough. So anyway some of the Dublin crowd were shouting to Ben "Give us a close free". I wouldn't say he gave it, but sure you wouldn't know what went on in the course of the game. There was another Galway goal and another goal from Dublin. It went on and on. I remember on one occasion Galway were really annoyed. I was stooping down to pick up the flag to put it up for a point. The referee, Ben, was waiting to see what I was going to do about it. I was only stooping down to put up the flag, and this fella came over and shouted at me to "Put up the f---ing flag". The point was for Galway. I wasn't going to let it go, it had to be right, the point was surely for Galway. Oh it was such a tense match.

Well, when the match was over anyway they all decided they were going to get the referee. I think Dublin won the match. And then Ben was taken away. The police came on the pitch to take Ben away. The crowd went wild. Well, Ben got garda protection down to the hotel, down to Hayden's Hotel. The police were on duty outside the hotel to give him protection; there was a crowd outside the hotel.

Someone said to Ben "If you don't get out of this town you're on your own". So they decided to put Ben in a car and put him out the Dublin Road while the police were still left outside the hotel. He went off in hiding. We picked him up later on in the evening, I don't know where. Sure Ben went into hiding.

The following Sunday, a month later, there was a match up in Belfast, I wasn't there but Ben was. Soon the word was out that Ben was seen at the match. The word came back of a conversation that someone had heard.
"Did you see who was up at the match in Belfast? Remember the fella who refereed the match in Galway?"
"Who the fella from Wicklow?"
"Yea, well, he was there. And he was all dressed up like a prized bull at the match and cheering for Dublin".

The Street Leagues

When I went to live in Cabra, I joined the Cabra Presidia of the Legion. They were thinking about doing something for the youth, maybe start a youth club. It was coming up to the summer period and I used to see young fellas playing ball on the street, there were a few hurley sticks around too. So I had the idea of organising and starting street leagues. I decided to put it to the Presidia meeting that we could start up street leagues.

That was accepted and so we went from door to door along the roads of Cabra. Our intention was to set up street leagues but Cabra had roads, so we set up road leagues. We went out in pairs, there was about eight of us involved. We knocked on the doors and informed the good ladies at the doors what we were all about. We were brothers from the Legion and we thought there was very little being done for the boys of the area and that we'd be delighted and satisfied if we could get road leagues going. If they worked we were going to run football and hurling leagues. We'd have two leagues to cater for all the boys: 12-14 years for the juniors and from 14 years-18 years for the seniors.

The first response was "Come in please, it's the best news I've got for a long time, its an absolutely fantastic idea." We got great praise for what we were doing and great encouragement to go on. One day borrowed another until we got teams going for various roads. We had lists of names. Hoggar, who was with us in the Legion, was a Department official, he worked in the Civil Service and he was able to get his hands on a typewriter so we got the lists of names all typed up.

And then people said "But where's the club?"
"We have a colossal club and we've no shortage of space" says one of our lads.
"Where? Will it be built soon?"
"No, its there all the time"
"Where?"
"It's in broad daylight – it's in the Phoenix Park. There's loads of space in the Park to play these games, and we will be manning them all, we have plenty of help to do that "

We had been going for a while and one evening we happened to meet Paddy O'Keeffe, secretary of the GAA at the time. He says "I want to compliment you and the others involved, you are so enthusiastic. We are getting great reports about Cabra being alive with street leagues, the road leagues." He finished up by saying that when we had gone through road playing road and the knock out competitions, when it came to the last four and if we were looking for a place he would have no problem giving us Croke Park.
"When it comes to the finals I promise you that" says he.

So O'Keeffe, rest his soul, kept his promise. We had our matches, all the play-offs, in the Phoenix Park. When it came to the match in Croke Park, we had it on a Sunday morning, at the end of September, after the All-Ireland finals had been played, it was around that time. Mick Daniels, captain of the Dublin hurling team of 1936, I think it was 1936, agreed to referee the matches in Croke Park. Army Metro was the name of Mick's club.

We had a great turn out; we had a great crowd of helpers as well. We gathered up and left from O'Connell St Bridge. The juniors were all dressed up wearing their jerseys. The seniors were dressed up in the colours.... Green? I'm not sure, now at this moment, what colours they were. But we left O'Connell Street Bridge anyway. We'd also contact with the Post Office Brass and Reed Band. They had said yes they would be able to muster enough to bring us down to Croke Park and play us around the ground. So that worked as well. Well, we left O'Connell Street Bridge and went down Milford Road and the lads and the people who were admirers whatever, went onto the pitch and paused for a while. The band then played us around the ground, and it took off from there. The band then went about its business. We had just got the promise that they would bring us down to, and around Croke Park, and they did that.

When the match was over there was great excitement and high jinks. The cup and the medals were presented to the lads by the national secretary of the GAA Paddy O'Keeffe. I think there was a priest with him, a Kerryman, I think he was a priest in Sundrive Road at the time, and he joined Paddy O'Keeffe for the presentation.

There had been a great turnout and we had a great evening. We followed through in the following year. We had something, which mightn't have been so big, but then we went on to different fields of activity. But we made a name for ourselves and after that we went to the GAA minor board and registered a team for Cabra parish. They played in the minor competition. We played matches all over the city. Some of the youngsters would have been so poor. I remember one Sunday we were drawn against a particular team and we were playing out in Killester Park. We had such a crowd from Cabra who turned up to see the kids playing. But there had been awful rain the night before, and the pitch was really wet. Well, those kids went out there, only in their runners. Well, to see those young lads, and they going up and down with their hurley sticks and they skiting water in all directions. I don't know if it was Vincent's that we were playing, but they were a very well known club, a famous club, supporting both juniors and seniors. But we were the poor Cabra lads. The result was anyway that we got on, and we got great credit for it, and as I said we were registered as members of the GAA minor board.

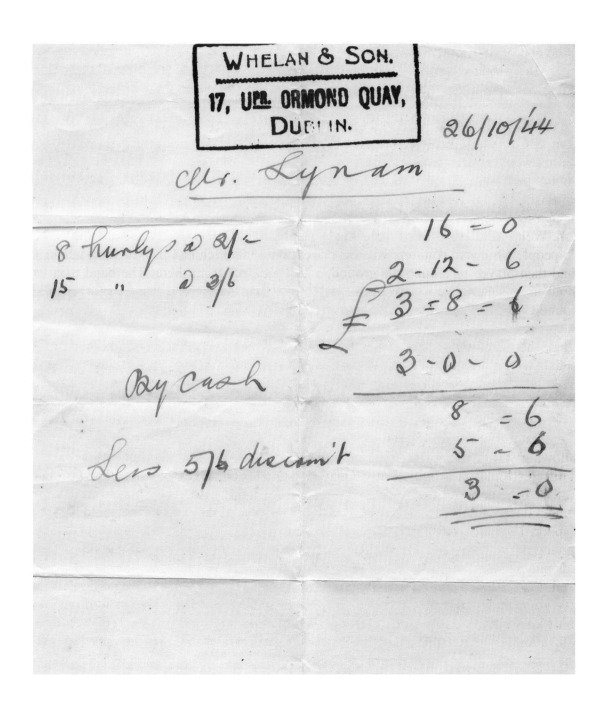

WHELAN & SON.
17, UPR. ORMOND QUAY,
DUBLIN.

26/10/44

Mr. Lynam

8 hurlys @ 2/-   16 = 0
15 "   @ 2/6   2 - 12 - 6
                    £   3 = 8 = 6

                        3 - 0 - 0

    Pay cash
                        8   = 6
    Less 5/6 discount   5 - 6

                        3 - 0

101	...	30/8/46	Annaly Road	v	Annamoe Park,	S. F.
102		31/8/46	Annamoe Drive, 1	v	Quarry Road,	J.F.
103	...	1/9/46	St. Attracta, 1	v	St. Eithne,	S.H.
104		2/9/46	Annaly Road	v	Leix Road,	S.F.
105	...	4/9/46	St. Attracta, 3	v	Erris-Fertullagh,	S.F.
106		5/9/46	St. Eithne Road	v	Leix Road	S.F.
107	...	6/9/46	Erris-Fertullagh	v	St. Jarlath,	S.H.
108		8/9/46	Annaly Road	v	Annamoe Drive, 2	S.H.
109	...	9/9/46	St. Attracta, 1	v	Quarry Road,	S.H.
110		11/9/46	Annamoe Drive, 1	v	Annamoe Park	S.H.
111	...	12/9/46	Annamoe Terrace	v	Annamoe Park,	J.F.
112		13/9/46	Dowth-NewGrange	v	Leix Road,	J.F.
113	...	14/9/46	St. Attracta, 1	v	Quarry Road,	J.F.
114		15/9/46	Annamoe Terrace	v	St. Attracta, 2	S.H.
115	...	16/9/46	Annamoe Drive, 2	v	St. Attracta, 2	J.F.
116		18/9/46	Annaly Road	v	Annamoe Terrace	S.H.
117	...	19/9/46	Annamoe Drive, 2	v	St. Attracta, 2	S.H.
118		21/9/46	Annamoe Drive, 1	v	Quarry Road,	S.H.
119	...	22/9/46	Annamoe Terrace	v	St. Jarlath	S.H.
120		23/9/46	Annamoe Drive, 1	v	St. Eithne	S.H.
121	...	25/9/46	Annaly Road	v	Dowth-NewGrange	S.H.
122		26/9/46	Annamoe Park	v	St. Attracta, 3	S.H.
123	...	27/9/46	Dowth-NewGrange	v	Erris-Fertullagh	S.H.
124		28/9/46	St. Attracta, 1	v	St. Eithne	J.F.
125	...	29/9/46	St. Eithne Road	v	Leix Road	S.H.
126		30/9/46	St. Attracta, 2	v	Dowth-NewGrange	S.H.
127	...	6/10/46	Annamoe Terrace	v	Dowth-NewGrange	S.H.
128		13/10/46	Annamoe Drive, 1	v	St. Attracta, 1	S.H.
129	...	20/10/46	Annaly Road	v	St. Attracta, 2	S.H.
130		27/10/46	St. Attracta, 1	v	St. Attracta, 3	S.H.
131	...	3/11/46	Annaly Road	v	Erris-Fertullagh,	S.H.
132		10/11/46	Annamoe Drive, 1	v	St. Attracta, 3	S.H.
133	...	17/11/46	Annamoe Terrace	v	Erris-Fertullagh	S.H.
134		24/11/46	Leix Road	v	Quarry Road	S.H.
135	...	1/12/46	Erris-Fertullagh	v	Fassaugh Road	S.H.
136		8/12/46	St. Eithne Road	v	Annamoe Park	S.H.
137	...	15/12/46	Annaly Road	v	St. Jarlath	S.H.
138		5/1/47	Annaly Road	V	Fassaugh Road	S.H.
139	...	12/1/47	Annamoe Park	v	St. Attracta, 1	S.H.
140		19/1/47	St. Attracta, 1	v	Leix Road	S.H.
141	...	26/1/47	St. Eithne	v	Quarry Road	S.H.
142		2/2/47	Annamoe Drive, 2	v	Erris-Fertullagh	S.H.
143	...	9/2/47	Annamoe Park	v	Leix Road	S.H.
144		16/2/47	Annamoe Drive, 2	v	Annamoe Terrace	S.H.
145	...	23/2/47	Annamoe Drive, 2	v	St. Jarlath	S.H.
146		2/3/47	Annamoe Drive, 1	v	Leix Road	S.H.
147	...	9/3/47	St. Attracta, 3	v	St. Eithne Road	S.H.
148		16/3/47	St. Attracta, 3	v	Leix Road	S.H.
149	...	23/3/47	St. Attracta, 3	v	Quarry Road	S.H.
150		30/3/37	Annamoe Terrace	v	Fassaugh Road	S.H.
151	...	6/4/47	St. Attracta, 2	v	Erris-Fertullagh	S.H.
152		13/4/47	St. Attracta, 2	v	St. Jarlath	S.H.
153	...	20/4/47	St. Attracta, 2	v	Fassaugh Road	S.H.

A section from the fixture list of the Cabra Road Leagues

The young lads from Cabra.

The Post Office Brass & Reed Band leading the finalists of
the Cabra Road Leagues around Croke Park.

May the best team win!

And there were no losers!

We would raise funds for the gear. There was no money asked of the youngsters or their parents. We were glad to have them and we'd raise money through running raffles and various things to keep the leagues and the club going. I don't know if we charged them going into Croke Park, I can't remember, but it was a surprise item anyway.

The people who came to Christ the King parish had suffered quite a bit, many of them came from the tenements in the north inner city, many of them came to Cabra from the North Strand, their houses would have been bombed and flattened in the Dublin bombs. And there was terrible poverty. People suffered very badly through the war, and there was no welfare.

There's one other thing that sticks out in my memory. I met two women standing on a corner on the road, one night we were going up to collect the boys. They knew we were going up to collect the boys, there was a match in the Park that night. I spoke with the two women as we passed by "Good evening, we are up to collect the boys, tonight we're playing such and such a road". And one woman turned to the other woman and said "Thanks be to God, that leaves us free for the night. I think we'll go to the pictures". "You" said the other woman to me, "Well, if you are around we know things are going to be all right, they will be with you up in the Park and there will be no problems. If we were to go out another night, there would be surely somebody who would misconduct themselves, and the whole road would get the blame for it".

This was Christ the King Parish; West Cabra hadn't started hurling at that stage. But West Cabra afterwards had teams entered in competitions; interested adults got the kids in West Cabra organised. Many of those young fellas that were in the road leagues went on and were successful in their lives; many of them became great soccer players too.

Well, we thought at the time that we could do a bit of good for the kids and for the area and it worked. I say its a pity, that at the time of the road leagues, there was many a hurler, and many a hurling team that came to Dublin, and with all respects to hurlers who would come from all over Ireland, they would come up to Dublin and they would come up with all their credentials and they would form teams and they would play in the senior or junior ranks, but they never saw the youth from the streets who were playing ball or marbles or whatever. But we thought we were doing that one better. And I'd say we did it because we believed we could do something for the less fortunate who were going to be.... well, whose talent wasn't going to be recognised. I just mention the hurlers coming to Dublin and forming a team and joining a team. Well, they were gaining by coming to Dublin. But if someone came to Dublin to spend some of their free time and do something for the poor of

Dublin, they would be giving something and they'd get something back too. I suppose we at that time were very enthusiastic about what we were doing.

There was real poverty; Dublin was a very poor city at the time. There was plenty of unemployment in Dublin at the time; there was nothing else. In the early 40's during the war, I happened to see one march. The unemployed were marching and carrying a coffin down Grafton Street. And I remember the unemployed were very strong but they weren't able to get much further. They were very powerful, they were well thought about in terms of standing up for themselves. At one stage they put up candidates for election. One person, I can't remember the man's name, got elected to the Dáil. But he only stuck it for about a month 'cause he wasn't able to carry on and speak for himself. He was up against it and he wasn't able to continue with it. Those were the sad days in Dublin.

My mother's illness and her death

I was in Dublin and I was asked by the others to visit and go and see the doctor, Dr. Quinlan, a big man, over there in Fitzwilliam Square. My mother was to have an operation, I know now that she had cancer. I remember going over to Fitzwilliam Square, I remember I felt I was just like a chicken, with all these other people going to see this famous Dr Quinlan. I remember waiting. And when it was my turn I just asked him - I spoke and told him who I was - I remember so well the building of the house and the size of the big room and all that, and exactly where he was standing. I just asked him and I said to him "I was asked from home to find out from you if this operation was serious" I remember that was the way I put it.
"Well, my dear boy, all operations are serious". And that was it, and he walked away. God, I remember I was knocked back.

But I do know at that time that Josie was working in Clanbrassil Street in a confectionery shop belonging to Mr Webster and Josie was very friendly with his wife and I think he was a Jew. He was very friendly visiting our house, he could spend a few days down on holidays and my mother would chat with him.

I do know and remember, Mother had agreed on the Friday evening to having the operation. She was in the small hospital on St Stephen's Green, St Vincent's, and she was all set for this operation. She had had her teeth taken out, because she was going for the operation. On the Monday evening, when I called in to see her, she said she had a change of plan. "I've changed my mind," she said. "I am not going to have the operation. Mr Webster was in last night and he advised me. So I am not going to have the operation". For me she took Mr Webster's advice. She said "Well, operations are uncertain and you don't know" and all that sort of thing. She said she thought she wouldn't have the operation and she would go home instead and "Sure anyway if I am to die, I will die at home with my children". "Who knows?" she said.

I still would have letters she wrote me all about that time. She would write "I was out today and I had a great day today. Aunt so-and-so and Aunt so-and-so called to see me and I walked out as far as the cup and saucer". And she'd say, "wasn't that great". That's how she lived out her life.

I'm not sure how long she lived after that visit to hospital in Dublin, but I did know that she wasn't well and anything was liable to happen. She was only in her fifties when she died in 1943[69].

I remember one Sunday evening, Rose was with me in Croke Park and we got a message, it had come by phone. The message was that we were to come home, that Mother was seriously ill. That was it. We got up the following morning and got the first train out of Dublin and down to see her and out to the County Hospital. And she seemed in good form. "Its only Monday, how did you manage to get free today?" she asked us.
"Well" I said, "the way it is in our place we get time off for our efforts".
Whatever I was going to tell her I wanted her to think it wasn't strange for us to be there. "We could get time off at anytime and sure we decided we might come down to say hello to you". I said something as light as that. She chatted us.

That same day in the hospital I remember my mother asking me to go over to Mrs Keenan. "Tom go over there to that bed there, and say hello to that woman and shake hands with her. That's the woman who saved all of you when you were very, very ill with the jaundice. It was her bottle that cured all you people and I'd like you to go over and say thanks".
I went over to Mrs Keenan's bed and thanked her. I remembered Mrs Keenan. I remember often going over to her after leaving school in Curraghmore to bring one of her bottles home. Mick Ryan and everyone around our whole area were cured with her bottle, her cure.

Later in the night I saw Fr. Glennon, a Franciscan from the Abbey in Multifarnham. He was a Glennon from Glennon's yard where we used to go hunker sliding on the ice. We knew him when we were going to school and he was studying then to be a Franciscan. My mother had great respect for the Franciscans.

---

[69] Mary Lynam (nee Loughrey) died on 25 May 1943.

I approached him; I wanted him to see my mother. After shaking hands with her, he talked with her for a while. I knew that made an awful difference to her to have had a visit from a Franciscan. I don't know if Josie was with me. Then Fr. Glennon asked me did I realise that my mother was very seriously ill. He evidently knew. She was on morphine all the time and the effect of the morphine was fading away. There was a nurse there all the time, a nurse from Mullingar and she was nursing Mother. Josie seemed to know her, 'cause Josie had the confectionery shop in Dominick Street at the time.

We asked the nurse how my mother was. "Well, I think she will last the night," said the nurse. So we decided to slip over as far as Dominick Street to where Josie had the shop for a cup of tea. We told the nurse we would then be straight back. But when we got back to the hospital after the tea, Mother had died. It was tough, tough, tough. Everyone really loved my mother.

It was awful I was so upset after my mother dying, and I remember someone saying, "We've no home in Marlinstown now 'cause Mother is gone".

There is one thing that I regret and that is not bringing my mother to Dublin. I had one wish for a while, for a long while and I couldn't afford it, and that was to bring my mother to Dublin. To save enough money to bring my mother to Dublin would have been a great feat and I would have been satisfied. I had intended to but it never happened. She went out of her way to look after me when I went to Dublin first. She would send me up money and she would never see me short of a shilling. But I wanted to be able to say "Mother it's my treat, it's my money and we are going to have a day out in Dublin". But I never got to it. It was sad at the time. Another thing about it is.... do you know the song "You'll never miss your mother till she's gone"?

> "A mother's love is a blessing,
> No matter where you roam.
> Keep her while she's living,
> You'll miss her when she's gone.
> Love her as in childhood,
> When feeble, old and grey
> For you'll never miss your mother's love
> Till she's buried beneath the clay".

It's a very nice song, a very good reminder for people. Whatever anyone else thinks, I think myself, that mothers are the backbone of the country, the backbone of the country, because they are there, and they will always be there.

Mr Cowley was at my mother's funeral. I remember him telling me to "Take it easy, just to take it easy", and that there was no rush on me coming back. He also said at the time if I wanted to bring the girls up to Dublin, he gave me the preference of bringing them up. Teresa came up later and worked with Treasa in Pidgeons in Inchicore.

Mary took over when my mother died; though since the time that she gave up school she was the mother of us all. She made cakes, she did everything, tubs of washing, she made a great breakfast in the morning, she would help with the milking, she would do everything. She gave everything to Marlinstown. And she was great for keeping tabs on everything. She would know everything that was going on. She would know about all the funerals and who should go and where they were on. She was always there, and at the forefront of everything.

Later Mary fell in love with Tom Dunne. They were two people the same, great people. We had such a great hooley in the barn in Banagher, the night they were married.

Recreation

But a lot of time went into making preparations and getting things sorted out. Life must go on like anything else. We had leisure in between. For recreation we went to the cinema, to camogie and hurling matches, and dancing. We went to Barry's, the Teachers, the AOH, the Galway Arms. They were all the ceili and old-time dance halls.

My life was like electric, I was moving all over the place. I moved from the digs with Mrs Casserley in Cabra to a flat with Rose and Teresa in Norfolk Road, in Phibsboro. Later we moved into a flat in Iona Road. That was with Ms Lenihan, she owned the house with her father. We rented the top flat. We were right across the road from the church. We could leave the flat, as the priest was leaving the sacristy, and we'd be in front of the altar at the same time. I remember cycling with Treasa from that flat in Iona Road to watch a match in Drogheda, that would have been about sixty miles up and back.

I think it was around that time too, that I bought a greyhound. That happened through the Cunninghams. Lilly looked after the dog for me over by Molly's house in Glasnevin. Lilly got me to join up St. Margaret's Coursing Club too, but I was too busy with other things. Lilly Cunningham was completely mad about greyhounds. She said to someone one day "When I go to mass on Sunday, sure I see the greyhounds jumping over the altar." My dog, I can't even remember the name of it, went to the track a few times but it was never any good.

Getting closer to Treasa

Any work Treasa was doing, I would have occasion to know about it. Then she got a term of work with me along with four other girls in the Coombe. She would be anxious in the evening time that she would finish early. She would have all her end of the shop done, and her cash register counted. But it was a known thing, at that time we had a rule in the business that everyone had to wait until all the registers were checked, independent of whether it was your register or not, and all had to wait till all the registers were checked. She would have to be hanging around and she used to get annoyed. "I'm not waiting any more to get those registers checked when I've mine done long ago."

So then Pidgeons opened a new branch out in Inchicore and Treasa was put in charge. So she went out to Inchicore to manage that branch, a small shop, herself and another girl. So that was that. I suppose we got closer sometime after that, when she was out in Inchicore and she was more on her own. She was always top of the class with her business. She drove us all mad. If Treasa was doing anything, she did it really well and if she would be doing anything, she would be always finished first. We'd be only tidying up in the Coombe in the evenings and she'd arrive in, her business done, her cash counted, arriving down on her bicycle after closing at the same time as us, but with all her cash done to the nines. And she full of beans too.

We used to do a weekly account then and take stock. You wouldn't have loads of stock in a small place, but we had in the Coombe, and, we had the stores too. I was manager in the Coombe, so I was busy enough and hadn't that much free time. But I remember on many occasions making arrangements to meet Treasa out in Inchicore. I'd go out to Inchicore and she would have my tea ready and set up, out at the back of the shop. She would have the keys and we might sit there for the night or go to the pictures. She made a grand tea; she never made a fuss. There might be an evening when I might have something on or might like to go somewhere and she'd say "Cancel it! Come out for your tea and we can chat". We weren't engaged at the time.

Dancing at the Gresham Hotel.

Souvenir Programme

Edward Lee & Co. Ltd.

ANNUAL

Staff Dance

1945

Metropole Ballroom

4th January

Committee

Chairman—Mr. Thomas Clancy

Joint Secretaries—
Miss H. O'Sullivan   Miss E. Fehily

Hon. Treasurer—Mr. Jas. Smyth

M.C.—Mr. G. Walsh

Miss M. Byrne   Miss M. Shortt
Miss M. O'Donohoe   Miss M. Somers
Miss A. Sutton   Miss E. O'Farrell
          Miss M. Lynam
Mr. M. Higgins   Mr. J. Fagan
Mr. T. Shortt   Mr. W. Burke

Programme of Dances

No.	Dance	Tune
1.	Foxtrot	Piccadilly Pastime
2.	Foxtrot	Shootin' a line
3.	Slow Waltz	You were right
4.	Foxtrot	The Canteen Bounce
5.	Old Waltz	Thousand-and-one Nights
6.	Paul Jones	Selected
7.	Slow Foxtrot	Time waits for no one
8.	Foxtrot	So dumb, so beautiful
9.	Tango	Ferando
10.	Rhumba	It's love, love, love
11.	Slow Waltz	Fascination
12.	Paul Jones	Selected
13.	Slow Foxtrot	It had to be you
14.	Foxtrot	Swinging on a Star
15.	Old Waltz	Selection Irish Airs
16.	Irish Dance	Walls of Limerick
17.	Slow Waltz	Rozenne
18.	Foxtrot	Milkman keep those bottles quiet
19.	Medley of Dances	Lambeth Walk, Conga, etc.
20.	Foxtrot	Atlantic Jive

NATIONAL ANTHEM

front (L-R) Brigid & Ben, Maire & Ciaran,

back (L-R) friends of Maire, Treasa & Tom.

When will we get married Treasa?

The 'suggestion' and talk of marriage in the Pine Forest on August Monday 1944

I remember the day Treasa and myself first talked about getting married. I knew at that stage that she would marry me, and she was the girl for me. It was only a question of when would we get married. I suppose I hadn't asked her out straight, but it was always leading that direction. Sure we were doing everything together, and going everywhere together, we were so busy. If she wouldn't have agreed that we should get married then, it would have been a big shock to me. So, as I said, the question was really about when would we get married? Treasa remembers that August Monday as the day that I first made the 'suggestion'. We had gone to the Pine Forest, for a picnic on our bicycles. Afterwards she wrote a little note on a photo of me that she had taken on that day. *"When T made his first suggestion...when we would get married"*.

The Grand Dances

Every big shop would have their annual staff dance, Switzer's, Lee's, the big houses. Well, Máire, Treasa's sister was working out in Bray in Lee's. Máire would have the Lee's staff dance and we would be out at that. A lot of her friends would be there and a lot of our friends would go too. We would be at the Lee's staff dance in the Gresham and another staff dance in the Metropole hotel, and that went on. The men would hire the suits; the women had the grand dresses or might make up a dress. We might get a lift with a fella or maybe all get a taxi. There were all sorts of dances, waltzes, quick steps, slow steps, fox trots, a great mix of everything.

Cycling around the country

During the holidays of 1944 Tom McSweeney, Cathal Walsh and myself went off on holiday. We were a bit like the three musketeers. We packed everything into the saddlebags of the bikes and took the bikes with us on the train to Cork. We visited all the sites in the city, of course we took loads of photos, I had one of my cameras with me. We went out to Blarney Castle and then cycled all the way through West Cork to Glengarriff. You heard me often turn down fresh salmon at a dinner, well, the only time I ever really enjoyed fresh salmon was that night in Glengarriff, at half past ten at night. The three of us arrived in on the three bikes and we were absolutely murdered with the hunger, and the tiredness. We were after cycling through West Cork all around by Inchigeelagh and Gougane Barra and other famous places. We had gone to the Poulgorm Hotel and found the hotel full. They directed us across the road. On the far side of the road there were about six or eight women sitting outside. We were to leave our bags into the hallway and the bikes outside. We were anxious to see what was on the menu, but the women were anxious to see what was on for the night. We pulled up trousers over the shorts and got the tea. It was absolutely gorgeous. When we were finished the tea we said we were hitting the sack, but, well, the women weren't hearing any of it, we were lads on our holidays.

Well, it was one of those places where the furniture could be pushed back against the wall and so we danced there for about three hours, all sorts of dances, sets and everything, we had a woeful night. The next morning there was a priest there from Mount Argus and the rule of the hotel was that he was saying mass at nine o'clock or ten o'clock and after that the women were off for the day. They wanted to know where we were going. We thought we would go over to Garnish Island. When we went up to the little slipway to take a boat, there were two boatmen and two boats.

"Do you want a boat sir, would you like a boat sir?" says one of the men.

Well, there were six of us and we would need a fairly big boat. But the question was "Who knows how to row?"

"Lynam knows how to row" says Tom. "Sure hasn't he all that experience as a young fella out on Lake Derravaragh that he's always told us about".

"Come on says I, there's nothing to it".

Anyway, McSweeney decided to be first in, always the hero, and then Cathal Walsh and the three women and myself. Well, we were about half way across the lake and there was like a mini island in the middle of the lake, and I slowed down the boat.

"Will I say something says McSweeney?"

"Say nothing at all" says I.

But up he got, and stood up tall in the middle of the boat, and you know the size of McSweeney. And the boat starting going like this and like that, swaying from side to side "I'll recite Robert Emmet's speech from the dock" say's he, with the arms outstretched.

Well we got over anyway. That's the photo of Garnish Island.

We got home anyway that night and spent a night in the hotel, I can't remember what craic was on that night. The next morning we got up and stuffed everything into the saddlebags, McSweeney had two bags on either side of his bike. I went out and paid the bill for the overnight and the food. It was very cheap anyway. The lads had everything strapped down on the bikes, and off we went. "How much did you pay?". Well, when they discovered how little it cost, they were mad at me for paying the bill and not coming back to tell them first. We could have stayed on and had another few days in Glengarriff, it was really great value.

We went from that into Kenmare and from that to Killarney and we cycled all around Killarney and up to Moll's Gap and all those places. We hired out ponies and went up into the gap, well, everyone does that. After Killarney someone said "Where are ye going?"

The Three Musketeers!

Tom on Patrick Street, Cork.

Tom and Tom McSweeney on the Ring of Kerry.

Tom McSweeney and Tom on Garnish Island.

Tom McSweeney and Tom in Gougane Barra.

Tom and Cathal Walsh on the Lakes of Killarney.

Milking in Newcastle West.

Brother Thomas Ignatius and Tom in Tralee.

(L-R) Pat, Tom, Jim with ponies & foals in the yard.

"To Galway!" But first we went to Newcastle West, we had our hair cut by two women hairdressers there, and we stayed around and we met up with Tom McSweeney's relations. Then we cycled to Limerick, saw the Treaty Stone and then headed for Galway. In Galway we stayed in Gibbons Hotel. The beds were so soft and McSweeney was delighted, he was pretty sore at that stage. Well, we went out to Salthill and all around and about.

We had decided that we were only staying in Galway for one night, and that we would head for Mullingar and spend a night or two in Marlinstown. Marlinstown was always full of pals. Mary was there at the centre of everything. It was a great life with people visiting always, there was always an open door. I was in Dublin and missed some of it, but I probably made up for it when I was down.

Well, we left Galway at a quarter past four in the afternoon and set off for Mullingar. I might have told you this bit of the story before. I remember it rang twelve o'clock at the Dublin bridge and we still had to go in to Marlinstown. When we finally got in home McSweeney fell down, he was nearly worn out.
"What's wrong with you?" says I.
"Lynam" says he, "I'm too hungry to eat and I'm too tired to sleep" and he went up stairs and into the bed. "Lynam come up here" he shouted down, and I went up and found him. And he was lost, sunk down in the height of feathers, in my mother's feather bed. It's as clear to me still. The two of us had a great sleep in that big bed that night.

It was a great holiday. We saw the country and we got burnt with the sun and roasted our backsides on the bicycles. God bless the women, they said, "Go enjoy yourselves".

The three of us, Cathal, McSweeney and myself had out photo taken together again, when we met up at Treasa's and my fortieth wedding anniversary.

A dapper dresser

I was never a dapper dresser, that's a joke. Men always wore suits, trench coats and hats. And I bought the Cromby coat long before I was married. It was a very popular coat, a lot of people wore crombies, they were in fashion at the time. It weighed a ton, but of course you would walk around in it, or cycle in it. It has never worn out, and it came in handy on many a bed, and was often put on the bed when you all were children.

Driving home for Christmas - in a motorcar

The year the war was settled, the year the war ended, the motor cars were all out. The boss asked me what I was doing for Christmas. "Don't say anything now, but when everything is settled down take one of the cars for Christmas. That was Tom Cowley, God Bless him, and I got that car on goodwill.

Before that our transport was ponies and drays, or ponies and spring carts - the little two-wheeled cart. Then we got six vans. Jimmy Daly had a shop in Dolphin's Barn, but at the same time he worked for Pidgeons. He had one of Pidgeons' vans that was easy to get at. The rest of the vans were under lock and key somewhere else. Mr Cowley told me to take Jimmy Daly's van. I decided to take Treasa home with me to Marlinstown.

Ben McDonald's uncle who lived in Harold's Cross gave him the loan of a car for Christmas, a Ford type car. Ben said that he would drive the car to Rockvale[70] if anyone wanted to go. So himself and Brigid and Vi (Vera) and Máire were going to go.

Treasa and Brigid were living in Rialto together, in a terrace of houses near the picture house. Vera, I think was visiting at the time. Máire of course was living in Bray and she came in on Christmas Eve to be ready to travel. People had ideas of taking parcels and boxes that they couldn't send in the post, so soon Ben had the car full of stuff, and filled up with boxes.

I took Vi and another person, and Treasa and myself in the van, we would be going as far as Kinnegad anyway. We started off and we told the others we would wait for them in Maynooth. Well, Ben's car stopped in Kilcock; of course I didn't know this. I pulled up about two miles from Maynooth as arranged. A man pulled up beside us in this car.
"Are you waiting for a car to come from Dublin?" says he "I have a message for you. The car that was following you has had a breakdown and has had a puncture".
I turned around and we went back on the Dublin road. When we got there Ben had already put on the spare, then stopped a car, got a lift and then gone and got the puncture fixed.

---

[70] Rockvale was Treasa's home place, near Boston and Tubber, Co Clare.

When he came back we put the wheel in the car and we were away in a hack. We probably lost an hour.

We headed off again and I don't know how far we got, when we had another stop. Ben had got another puncture. Something else happened then and he got another puncture. At this stage he got two new wheels, 'cause he was having so many problems with the two old wheels that he had. We thought there can't be much wrong now, everything was OK and everything was sorted. We kept in tow with them. At the Downes there was another stop. It had taken a whole day to get that far.

They were nearly ready to walk from there. But there was no such chance of getting to Clare at that point. If they could get as far as Marlinstown, we'd be in clover.

Ben and the lot of them, and the car, finally made it into our yard in Marlinstown. The first thing Brigid wanted to do was to ring Gort and say they'd had a mishap, the car had broken down. They were going to stay in Marlinstown for the night and instead of getting there for Christmas Day, they would get there on Stephen's Day. So we put them all up for the night in Marlinstown on their way to Clare.

I don't know if they got to Rockvale. I think they made it and then came back to Dublin the following day, though I can't be sure if they really went to Clare or just tried to get back to Dublin. In fact, I think the women travelled down by train in the end. But I do know the way it finished up with the car though.

Ben left the car below in a field in Kilcock on the way back. He rang up your man, his uncle, who gave him the car. He told him his car was in such and such a field in Kilcock and if it was of any use to him, he could go down himself and take it. And he told him that the keys were in such and such a place "cause I don't ever want to see them, ever again". Poor Ben, and there had been such excitement about going.

Do you know what happened the car? Well, do you know how long the Second World War lasted? 1939 to 1945, that's what? Six years? Well, the car was immaculate and everything looked brand new but the car hadn't been driven for six years. There were new tyres on it, everything was new on it, six years earlier, but now at this stage they were rotten, poor Ben was left with rotten tyres though everything looked immaculate.

PLANNING OUR FUTURE TOGETHER, TREASA AND I

Well, we were going around together for so long that everyone was wondering were we ever going to make a move. Treasa was wondering and I was wondering were we just taking this thing for granted and we decided we better start doing something about it.

We started looking around at houses to buy and getting information about houses. There was a nice house that we looked at up at Rialto bridge, and another one up at Dufferin Avenue bridge. Other people that we knew started to get serious about getting married too.

I don't remember exactly when we got engaged, 'officially', as you would say, but I remember the occasion. I gave Treasa a gold watch as an engagement present. She was happy, and showing the watch off everywhere. There weren't many flush jewellers then for buying rings, but Ganters we thought was very reliable. That's where we got the engagement ring and the wedding ring later.

We would often go over on a Sunday evening for our tea to Merrion Row, to O'Donoghue's. Aunt Dotie used to really like us to come over whenever Paddy was finished so that we could have tea together.   Well, I remember being over in Aunt Dotie's for our tea and there was great excitement in Merrion Row with the engagement ring.

We met every night coming home. It was like the full stop at the end of the night. Treasa would be doing Legion work and I'd be doing something else and we'd meet up at a particular time at the Broadway Cinema, they had a nice restaurant there and Treasa and I used to go and have tea and crumpets. I remember one night it was lashing rain. Treasa was living in Rialto at the time and she had on her good shoes. Well, when we got out of the restaurant and up to O'Connell Bridge, she took off her shoes and put them in the back of the bike and cycled home in her bare feet.

We were clear about what we really wanted to do. We wanted to marry and we also wanted to go into business together. The result was we began looking around at shops. There were half a dozen shops that we looked at. I'd look at them, and Treasa would always be interested in looking at them herself, in finding out for herself what was on offer, because she was as anxious as I was that we would make the right decision. When Treasa got serious, she was serious, in her head there was a straight road ahead and there was no break off that road.

I told Mr Cowley what I was intending to do. Some bosses mightn't be happy that you were going into business. Well, I was OK with Mr Cowley, I could talk to him. He was always of the opinion that I wasn't going to walk out of the Coombe. I was manager of the Coombe. There was no question of doing that, I couldn't afford to.

Acquiring the Shop The Pinnacle, No 28 Ring Terrace Inchicore

We decided to rent the shop in Inchicore... it was about a year before we got married. I rented the shop from a Mrs Hyland. She lived in Blackrock. We didn't have much money. We wouldn't need a lot of money, but we needed a loan. We felt we needed a bit of money to survive and get on, and I asked the boss. He told me to go up to the bank and everything would be OK, there would be no problem. He went guarantor for me. I got a loan from the bank for £100. That was to help stock the shop and to get us going. The boss went up before I took on the shop and had a look at it. Joe Shine went up as well, to see what it looked like before I finally took the place. They were my two bosses. The two, after seeing the place, told me I shouldn't have any problems. "You're doing the thing wisely. I think you'll make a go of it." That was good to hear from the boss.

And there was no question of setting up in opposition; ours was a small shop. But some people would wonder if there was a question of 'divided interest'? People would wonder about a fella that would be buying a business of his own, that he would set up and build up while he was managing another man's business. "Which should he, or would he, give the loyalty to?" Well, I didn't have any trouble in sorting that out.

I stayed on in the Coombe for a year, maybe two years after. Treasa started the shop on her own. She ran the shop with Sheila. She had the contacts and all my contacts, the people I got stuff from, and the managers all called. Treasa planned and stocked up the shop. She would need no help from anyone to organise the shop and most of the stuff. She soon built up the business. Everything was sold in the shop, needles, thimbles, hams, turkeys, buttons, biscuits, epsom salts, sausages, rashers, anything that you could or would ever need. I was manager in the Coombe as I said but every evening I would go up to Inchicore to help her. It would just tell you what a low standard of living there was. We rented the shop by the week. The entrance to the house was through the shop. There was a small room behind the shop with a gas cooker in the corner, there was no table and Treasa and Sheila would pull down the drop-leaf door of the press to eat the dinner. There was a toilet out in the back yard and two rooms upstairs over the shop. There was a shed in the back yard, there was about a ton of muck in it and the leftovers of rotten old potatoes. There were all sorts of things that we couldn't do, because we were only renting. The landlady was responsible for the outside and we could make a few changes inside.

We got married, I'm not sure how long after. But before we got married we had to do up the house in Inchicore, papering the rooms, decorating, whatever it took. It was very simple, it was very simple. The house was there, the rooms were there, it took a lot – well, I couldn't say it took a lot to get it done once you got stuck into it. I paid a fella from Kavanagh's of New Street to come with a truck to dig out and take away a truckload of rubbish and rotten potato from the shed in the back.

If I was anxious, Treasa was doubly anxious. But we had one thing in mind -that we were going to make a life out of it[71]. I was living in 37 Drumcondra Park when we rented Inchicore and I would go over at night to help out, painting and decorating or whatever. The result is you wouldn't have any idle time around the place. We would be working away till all hours at night in Inchicore. Treasa would often say "Do you really have to go back to Drumcondra on the bike? Would you not stay and go into to work from here in the morning?" I remember one miserable night getting a puncture at Kilmainham Jail and I walked all the way to Drumcondra pushing the bike.

Sheila and Treasa were great pals, they got on great and they worked really hard. They enjoyed the customers and the customers enjoyed them, and they had great sport too. Till this day some of the old customers that I meet in Inchicore still ask about Sheila. We had no car and no transport other than the bicycles. There was a little two-wheeled trolley to move heavy things around like sacks of potatoes and to deliver the orders to the customers. But there was no holding Treasa back, and Sheila was full of energy too. I remember hearing of the day Sheila went down on the bus with a big blue suitcase to get Chivers jellies, somewhere down off George's Street. She could hardly carry the weight of the suitcase full of jellies as far as the bus stop in Dame Street. But when she got it onto the bus the only thing she was worried about was that the jellies would burst out of the suitcase all over the floor of the bus and she would die of embarrassment.

The shop was one of three that stood alone on Ring Terrace, and at the time, beyond the back lane there was nothing but cabbage fields and allotments. Dan Wall's was the shop next door, Paddy Scally was working there. Sheila did a line with Gerry Farrell for a while, a pal of Paddy's. Later Paddy took over Wall's shop and married Nora, we were always the best of friends.

---

[71] It wasn't till later on, till after we married and the children started coming, that I built on the back kitchen and extended the shop. It was difficult, nearly impossible to get permission from the landlády to make changes inside the shop and living accommodation.

Treasa and Sheila in 1941.

For the fun at the fair. Bray 1943.

Sunshine and smiles and a touch of shyness. Sheila and Maire at the back of the shop in Inchicore.

Monday 4th August 1947.
(Photo Irish Press)

After the Wedding Ceremony, St. Michael's Church, Inchicore.
(Photo Irish Press)

Tom, Treasa, Fr. Healy, Maire, Pat.
(Photo Irish Press)

The Wedding Party.
(Photo Irish Press)

I remember the winter before Treasa and myself got married; it was a really bitterly cold winter. Fuel was really scarce. Sheila talks of seeing children with a pram full of turf for the fire and the water pouring down the side of the pram, the turf was so wet, it would be pure useless for making a fire. Treasa and herself used to burn the cardboard trays from the egg boxes for a blast of heat before they went to bed some nights. The eggman was never too pleased, they were supposed to return the large wooden eggbox, as well as the cardboard trays when they got their next order of loose eggs. When it was icy the two of them used to go out sliding on the street in the evening with the kids to keep themselves warm. They did it for the craic too I think. The two of them were always so full of sport and devilment.

The big day

And then we decided we would have the big day. And then it was all questions "When?" and "Where are we going to get married?" and "What hotel will we go to?" Well, we weren't well up on organising weddings; we weren't in the habit of going to weddings. It was our first time anyway, thanks be to God for that. We set the date for August Monday, it was four years to the day since I first made the 'suggestion' that we might get married.

We got married in St Michael's Church in Inchicore at seven o'clock in the morning on Monday the 4th of August 1947. Well, I was at the altar first, I was over in plenty of time to the church and Treasa was that little bit late, as was her privilege. And I remember Treasa kneeling beside me and leaning over to me and whispering in my ear.
"Tom are you nervous?"
Sure I whispered to her, "Say your prayers".
Well, she always told everyone, Lord rest her soul since, "That was the first salute he had for me - Say your prayers". She repeated what I said to everyone, but she was the apple of my eye, and always was, thanks be to God, my darling girl from Clare.

Fr. Brady and Fr. Healy married us. Pat, my brother was our best man. Máire, Treasa's sister was our bridesmaid. Pat had come up from Mullingar to stay with me the night before. I was living in Drumcondra Park and we slept together in the one room. We were up early and went over to the church by taxi. Mrs Mullally, my landlady in Drumcondra Park, gave me half a gold sovereign as I went out to the wedding that morning. The other chap in the digs in Drumcondra Park by the name of Clifford was a tailor, and he had made my wedding suit.

Treasa was in '28' in Inchicore with Sheila and Máire and Vi. It was an early start for everyone. Cars had been arranged to collect the priests and to bring the main party to the church.

Our families and friends were there, many of them travelled through the night to be there, my brothers, Jim and Bill and Pat and Mary Teresa, and sister Josie and Brian and young Richie, Rose and Eugene, Mary and Tom Dunne, and Teresa. Treasa's sisters Sheila, Máire of course and her boyfriend Ciaran Lehane, Vi, Brigid and Ben, and Treasa's brother Joe were there. Anna was in America then. My uncle Thomas Ignatius, the Christian Brother, was there, and there was Tom McSweeney, Flor and Seamus Lynam, Aunt Dotie, Carmel O'Donoghue and Paddy O'Donoghue, Elsie Cruise, and Veronica Dowd who worked with Máire in Lee's as well and Jimmy McCarthy, a captain in the army. There were a few others as well but the names fail me at the moment, isn't that shocking. A photographer was there from the Irish Press.

We had the mass and the wedding ceremony, and after the photographs were taken outside the church, we went down to the Parkgate Hotel on Parkgate Street, for the wedding breakfast. It wasn't an Irish breakfast, we had a meal, I can't remember now what exactly we ate. Of course there were the speeches, and I said my bit, and then we had the cutting of the wedding cake.

We were going to Cork and then Kerry for our honeymoon and we were travelling on the morning train. Well, when we came out of the hotel to go by car to Kingsbridge Station, Tom McSweeney, always as wild as a hatter, had all sorts of tin cans, and buckets and prams and more buckets tied to the back of the car. 'Just married' was written on the back too. They nearly called the fire brigade; there was so much noise in the area. Tom McSweeney was behind it, you would just have to look at the photographs and see Tom McSweeney's face to see that.

A great crowd came over to the train station to see us off. We were so happy. It was fantastic.

Honeymoon

We went to Cork on our honeymoon. We travelled by train and stayed in the big hotel in Cork, the Victoria, it was *the* hotel in Cork at the time. Nothing but the best for us. I remember we couldn't get the confetti up off the floor when we took off our overcoats in the hotel in Cork. God almighty save us, people in the hotel didn't know who they had, but they weren't long finding out when they saw all the confetti, there was a trail running after us. We walked around the quays that night. I was really tickled by the singing of the newspaper sellers, and the tune they had on the names of the evening papers, they sure had a tune of their own.

On top of Blarney Castle.

Newspaper seller outside Victoria Hotel Cork.

Killorglin Puck Fair.

Killorglin Puck Fair.

Riding through the Gap of Dunloe.
(Photographer unknown)

Leaving Killarney and heading home.

We visited Blarney Castle and kissed the Blarney Stone, we went to Blackrock castle. We went to Cobh; it was still called Queenstown then. We thought that was a very strange place. It was just a cold, cold place and we were told that so many people, heartbroken, left this quay and so many people, heartbroken, left that quay to go to New York, the stories that you are told and read about. I could see no life in the place at all. The cathedral was up on the hill. I thought it was a strange place Cobh. We stayed in Cork for three or four days and then we went off to Killarney.

We stayed for a week in Killarney and we cycled around. I can't remember where we got the bikes. We did a grand tour one day too. On Friday 8th August we did the 'Killarney tour No 1, 10.15am -6.45pm'. I know that 'cause later, Treasa put the details on the back of the photos. We went through the Gap of Dunloe on ponies, then took an eighteen-mile boat trip on the upper, middle and lower lakes to Ross Castle and then went by sidecar back to Killarney.

What was great about the honeymoon was that we were enjoying everything together.

We had a grand time in Killorglin and of course the Puck Fair was on at the time. Some things I wouldn't get over-excited about but I enjoyed and had a great interest in the fellas trying to get a penny into a basin. The lads that had set up the trick were paying 'two to one' if your penny, a large old penny, landed in the basin. You'd have to stand back the distance before you could have your go. It was a quart size basin, fairly shallow. People were throwing up their pennies and they were landing all around the basins. A big lot of them of course were landing first in the basins but then bouncing out. The lads were raking in a fortune. Well, I watched one fella for a while who had got the knack. It was a tarmacadam road and this fella would throw his penny and hop the penny about a foot this side of the basin. The penny would hit the road, would bounce, and then, hop into the basin. Of course, after a while they were paying out so much money to this fella, they were trying to get him to stop playing 'cause he had already won a fistful of money. "Now, now, let someone else play. Give someone else a chance to win some money". But even at that people didn't come along and say 'Ah that's the secret, now I have it'. I played my pennies for a while and I got 'two to one'. It wasn't quite a fistful of money, but it was good craic.

Coming home to Dublin

Coming back from the honeymoon, well, we were going to take each day at a time. I do know that we felt the holiday was over. There was that sort of feeling. We were both working. But we were both, blest born, that both of us had the one interest from the point of view of earning a living. You take a fella and a girl, say she's working in an office and he might be working his back off, and he'd wonder if she'd be pleased. But Treasa and I were working off each other, as it were. We were in the same line. I would hate to marry someone who knew nothing about business. My God you'd have some job then.

The one thing we knew, that we both knew, was that we could make a living together. It didn't matter whether she or I had gold teeth or a nice smile, as they used to say in the country long ago, "Those smiles won't boil a kettle".

Treasa was, I've said this a thousand times... well, there was no person that ever put clothes on their back, that could match Treasa in business. She'd be always on a joke, she would never take you seriously, but in business she was a real topper. As far as business was concerned, she was absolutely brilliant. And she was never in any way overpowering. She was brilliant at dealing with the public, she was really very popular with the customers, she was brilliant dealing with the finances, she had a great memory, she was sharp and quick and a great business head. She was so capable; she could do so many things. And she was always so giving; she was absolutely thrown away with kindness.

When I think back on our wedding day

When I think back on the wedding day, and I thought it then in the church, we were two people there, together, getting a sacrament. We were in God's hands. He decides, he holds the key, he holds the advice, he holds everything, but it is up to us. And we were getting then, all that the church could give us, from the point of view of a blessing. And I accepted that.

I was always a bit quiet, but if I was acting a bit quiet, Treasa would be in her element and she'd tease me, and joke. Like at the altar when she asked me if I was nervous. She was always full of devilment, on the ball and full of go. I remember after the wedding, I don't know if it was one of her own family that said to me "God Lynam, we didn't think you would ever tame her". A lot of people thought that. She had great spirit.

If I tried to find a hair's breath of a difference between us, anywhere down the line, I don't think I could find it. We got on so well. We were up to our ears in activity, with the Legion and the Vincent de Paul and the camogie and Croke Park, our life was full of sporting activity. I think I still have above in the garage, a bicycle that Treasa bought, before we were married. She bought it at the back of Hell's Kitchen in a little street above Camden Street going towards the canal. She bought it as a new bike, for two pounds four shillings and six pence[72]. That's the bike she rode around the country and when we did all our cycling together.

In the latter end of her days, Treasa would be always looking to take second place for herself. I used to say, "Treasa, God is listening to you."
"Tom", she'd say, "Tom, if it wasn't for you".
I would say, "Treasa, that is not true, it was never like that".
I surely loved her, I surely did.

We went around together before we married, we were going around together after we married, we loved each other and we were the best of friends, and there was no decision that we didn't make together.

Ah love, what is love? Love, it's so different today.

Love it is a funny thing,
It catches the young and the old.
It makes your tender heart feel,
Like a fresh water eel,
And it causes your head to swell.
It alters your mind,
For love it's so kind,
And it empties your pockets as well.

So boys keep away, from the girls I say,
And give them lots of room.
For when you wed,
They will bang your head,
With the bald headed end of a broom.

It must be over sixty years since I heard that one.

---

[72] Two pounds four shillings and six pence is equivalent to €2.22.

The stories after we got married? And rearing our family ... another book?
Well, let's take one day at a time.

And now my friends go if you will,
And visit other nations,
But leave your heart in Erin still,
Amongst your poor relations.

That spot of earth that gave you birth,
Resolve to love forever,
For you'll repent that good intent,
Oh never, never, never.

Go point me out on any map,
A match for green Killarney,
Kevin's bed, Dunloe's Gap,
Mystic shades of Blarney.

Antrim's caves, Shannon's waves,
Ah me, I doubt if ever,
An isle so fair was seen elsewhere,
Oh never, never, never.

Patrick Lynam's Will

I, Patrick Lynam of Marlinstown, in the County of Westmeath, farmer, do make this my last will and thereby revoking all former wills by me, if any heretofore made. I make the following deposition of the property I may die possess

I give to my wife £20 out of the amount which will be received on the policy of insurance on the life of Cathworth Ferguson Esq. I also give to my wife the right to live in my house here in Marlinstown and to be supported out of the profits of the old farm in Marlinstown during her life, and if she wishes to leave the place I will that she should be paid in annuity of £15 pounds per annum out of said farm. I leave my daughter Elizabeth £20. I leave to my daughter Ann £100 to be paid on attaining 25 years of age, or on her marriage with the consent of her mother under that age. I leave my son Michael £20 to be paid when he reaches 35 years of age. I leave to my son Thomas £20. I leave to my son Thomas and my daughter Ann the right to live in my house and to be supported out of the profits of the farm until they respectively reach 25 years of age[73] or until her marriage under that age in the case of Ann, but on condition that they especially shall give his or her labour on the farms free of charge subject to foregoing as the payments of my debts, funeral and testamentary expenses. I leave the residue of my property as follows viz. I leave to my son Patrick the farm I have purchased from my brothers widow in Marlinstown except the bog field containing two acres and I also leave him the field of my old farm called the Furze Hill and containing three acres or thereabouts and I direct that the proportion of the rent he shall pay be increased one pound sterling I leave my home farm and the bog field of the purchased farm before mentioned to my son William his proportion of the rent to be reduced by the pound which I have placed on the other farm I leave the residue of my property of every kind to my sons Patrick and William as to one third to Patrick and as to two thirds to William but the debts funeral and testamentary expenses to be paid by them in the same proportions I direct that neither of my said sons Patrick or William shall marry before William reaches thirty three years of age except on the written consent of their mother if they or either of them marry before said period and without such consent I direct that they or he as the case may be shall thereupon forfeit all rights under this will and the share bequeathed to the son on marrying shall go to my son Michael Lynam I appoint my wife Anne Lynam and my son William Lynam Executors of this my will As witness my hand this thirty first day of August one thousand eight hundred and ninety six *Patrick Lynam*

---

[73] Thomas joined the Christian Brothers at the age of 16 years.

Notes[74]

The gross value of Patrick Lynam's personal estate on his death on 10/06/1899 amounted to £1021-13-2 and estate duty of £3-0-2 was paid.

The name Lynagh (Patrick's family name and the name of his father) seems to have been changed to Lynam between Patrick's marriage to Anne Keenan and his death. He was registered as Lynagh at his marriage.

Patrick Lynam and his brother Tom went to America and returned around 1862 and leased 136 acres 0 roods 6 perches in Marlinstown Co Westmeath.

---

[74] These notes accompany the Lynam Family Tree prepared by Robert Cullen who lives in Ennis Co Clare. Robert is also a descendant of Patrick Lynam.